# FOOTBALL INJURIES

by
## MUIR GRAY

D1584871

# Edward Arnold

N 0162492 X

© Offox Press 1980    59 Lakeside Oxford OX2 8JQ

This edition first published 1982 by Edward Arnold (Publishers) Ltd,
41 Bedford Square, London WC1B 3DQ by arrangement with Offox Press

*All rights reserved. No part of this publicaton may be reproduced, stored in a retrieval
system, or transmitted, in any form or by any means, electronic, mechanical,
photocopying, recording, or otherwise, without the prior permission of Edward Arnold
(Publishers) Ltd.*

## DEDICATION

This book is dedicated to those thousands of people who give up their
spare time to coach, train, manage and help organize football without
any financial reward. Sport adds an extra dimension to the lives of
young people but the dedication of older people is necessary for the
game of football to flourish and for young people to enjoy it because
without the unpaid organizers the game would wither away.

**British Library Cataloguing in Publication Data**

Gray, Muir
    Football injuries.
    1. Soccer — Accidents and injuries
    I. Title
    617'.1027    RC1220.S5/

    ISBN 0–7131–0848–7

Typeset by Oxford Publishing Services, Oxford
Printed in Great Britain by Billing and Sons Ltd., Worcester
Illustrations by Peter Acty

# CONTENTS

NEWMAN UNIVERSITY
COLLEGE
BARTLEY GREEN
BIRMINGHAM B32 3NT

CLASS 617.1027
BARCODE 0 62492X
AUTHOR GRA

FOREWORD BY BOBBY MOORE
ACKNOWLEDGEMENTS
PREFACE BY JIM ROSENTHAL

## 1. THE MANAGEMENT OF FOOTBALL INJURIES

| | |
|---|---:|
| Taking control of injuries | 1 |
| The crucial decisions | 2 |
|   Timing | 2 |
|   Urgency | 2 |
| How to use this book | 3 |
| The Golden Rules | 4 |
|   Play Safe | 4 |
|   Play it Cool | 4 |
|   Look and Listen Before you Touch | 5 |
|   Prevention is Better than Cure | 6 |

## 2. PRINCIPLES OF TREATMENT    7

| | |
|---|---:|
| Psychological aspects of injury | 7 |
| Structure and function | 8 |
| Control of bleeding | 10 |
| Rehabilitation | 12 |
| Supportive strapping | |

## 3. THE INJURY TEAM    17

| | |
|---|---:|
| The Red Cross, St. John's and St. Andrew's | 17 |
| Physiotherapists and Remedial Gymnasts | 18 |
| Chiropodists | 19 |
| Dentists | 20 |
| Osteopaths and Chiropractors | 21 |
| Pharmacists | 22 |
| Doctors | 22 |
| The Football Association | 23 |

4. PREVENTION THROUGH TRAINING    25

Prevention through skill    25
Prevention through fitness    25
  Muscle fitness    26
  Heart-lung fitness    27
    Glucose supply problems    29
      Deficiencies    29
      Surpluses    30
    Oxygen supply problems    32
      Improving the muscle cells    34
    Training in principle and practice    34
      The loading principle    34
      Pulse counting and stopwatching    34
Fitness training for boys    37


5. SKIN WOUNDS    39

Prevention of skin injuries    39
  Accidents?    39
  Protecting shin and ankle    39
  Prevention of abrasions    40
  Groundsmen and Referees    40
Principles of treatment    41
  Cleaning and disinfection    41
  Tetanus    43
Practical treatment    43
  Cuts    43
  Puncture wounds    45
  Abrasions    45


6. MUSCLES AND TENDONS    47

Muscle injuries — tears, pulls and strains    48
  Strapping    50
Achilles tendon injuries    50
Prevention of muscle injuries    51
  Warming up    52
  Loosening up    53
    Quadriceps (thigh muscles)    53

Hamstrings 54
Calf muscles 55
Adductors (groin muscles) 57
Steaming up 58
Stiffness 58
Cramp 59
Calf cramp 59
Hamstring cramp 60
Foot cramp 61
Contusion — dead leg 61

7. FOOT PROBLEMS 63

Preventive foot care 63
The individual's contribution 63
The coach's contribution 64
Blisters 64
Athlete's foot 65
Verrucas and Corns 66
Painful feet 66
Acute pain 66
Chronic pain 67

8. ANKLE AND LEG INJURIES 71

The mortice and tenon joint 71
Inversion injuries 73
Assessment and early management 73
Returning to action 75
Pott's fracture 77
Chipped ankle bones 79
Broken legs 79
Prevention 80

9. KNEE INJURIES 81

Basic anatomy 81
Ligaments 81
Tendons 81

Muscles 84
Acute pain 84
Kicks 84
Torn ligaments 85
Torn cartilages 86
Quadriceps rehabilitation 88
Knee strapping 89
Chronic pain 89


10. SHOULDERS AND HANDS 91

Shoulder Injuries 91
Acute pain 91
Chronic pain 92
Hand injuries 92
Don't forget the Goalkeeper 93


11. VULNERABLE AREAS 96

Head injuries 96
Brain damage 96
Blows to the face and nose 98
Mouth injuries 98
Frontal blows 99
Uppercuts 99
Dental problems 100
Broken teeth 100
Avulsed teeth 100
Eye injuries 100
Dirt and mud 100
Cuts 101
Disturbance or loss of vision 101
Contact lenses 101
Breast injuries 101
Testicular injuries 102
Abdominal pain 103
Chest pain 103

## 12. PRE-MATCH PREPARATION     104

**Friday night**     104
    **Late nights**     105
    **Hangovers**     105
    **Sleeplessness**     106
    **Sex**     106
**Saturday morning**     106
    **Pre-match nutrition**     106
    **Half-time and extra time**     107
    **Fitness tests**     108

## 13. PREPARATION FOR INJURY MANAGEMENT     109

**The Treatment room**     109
**The Treatment bag**     109
**Aspirin and Paracetamol**     112
**Suppliers**     113

## 14. FINAL WHISTLE     114

# ACKNOWLEDGEMENTS

It is impossible to name everyone who has helped in the creation of this book, but certain individuals merit special mention. A number of professional colleagues read parts of the text on subjects about which they knew much more than I. Bill Bradshaw, Hung Cheng, Sam Galbraith, John Lourie, Gus McGrouther and Archie Young gave invaluable comments on the material relating to the management of injury, and Mrs Margaret John criticized constructively the section on physiotherapy.

I would also like to thank those who organised and, equally important, those who attended the seminars for and through which this material was developed.

I would like to thank in particular Tom McGarrity, who has taught me more about football and football injuries than he appreciates. His skill and experience are equalled only by his modesty.

All these people have helped. If this book is thought to have any good points, the credit should go to them and to my teachers at medical school. If the book has any deficiencies, they are entirely my responsibility. I have used 'the editorial we' throughout, but I alone am reponsible for the information presented in the book, and its shortcomings are the result of my shortcomings. The information and advice in the book is as accurate and as safe as is possible in a work of this length. Neither the author nor the publisher can accept any liability for any injury resulting from the reader's interpretation and application of the advice given.

MG

# FOREWORD

It has always been a bone of contention of mine that not enough has been, or is being done either to alleviate or treat injuries at the lower levels of football.

I have always felt there is a need for more professional advice on sporting injuries, particularly football injuries. Dr Muir Gray has written this enlightening and very informative book and aimed it at the layman, which is obviously essential because of the number of football teams playing in this country which operate with untrained managers or trainers. The book will also considerably help the senior clubs, particularly senior non-League clubs that are not fortunate enough to have professional staff to help them with their injury problems. The responsible attitude and outlook that Dr Muir Gray has on injuries is vital when one considers that to mistreat a particular injury could cause an injured player much suffering or perhaps permanent disability. The writer deserves every success with this book.

In my opinion it is long overdue and I feel sure it will be of tremendous benefit to the thousands of people who are involved in sport, particularly football, from the very junior level of the boys' game right the way through to the most senior of teams.

Bobby Moore

# PREFACE

'Stay on and run it off.' 'Come off and soak it in cold, no, hot water.' 'Immobilise your leg — no, try and keep walking.' 'You want an ice pack on that, or should it be the painkilling spray?'. . . .

Anyone who's been injured on the football field — and that means just about everyone who's ever played the game, has had the benefit of this sort of well-meaning, but often misguided and potentially dangerous advice. For every Malcolm Macdonald — forced to retire prematurely from first-division level — there are thousands of less gifted players who have been deprived of the pleasure of playing by incorrectly treated injuries.

If you are a million-pound player like Trevor Francis, the best treatment is instantly available. Despite our weekend delusions, most of us don't fall into the category — and yet the injuries are the same. Trevor Francis could have severed his Achilles tendon on any park-pitch in Britain; how many of us would have known what to do?

This book removes that combination of fear and helplessness which many of us have felt when a fellow player is hurt. The illusion of the all-curing magic sponge has gone forever. Here we have a clear, practical guide covering the complete range of football injuries.

Take it with you whenever you're in action. I hope you don't need to use it — but I'm sure you will.

Jim Rosenthal

# 1.
# THE MANAGEMENT OF FOOTBALL INJURIES

## TAKING CONTROL OF INJURIES

The key to football success is control. The player must be able to control the ball, and his emotions. The team must be able to control the game, and their ability to do that is due not only to the skills of the players but to the control which the manager, trainer and coach has over them between games. It is true that there are many aspects of the modern game in which there is too much control. Teams of young boys are coached and controlled as though they were professionals and some of the professional teams themselves play a controlled type of game which is often successful but which is frequently dull. But there is one aspect of the modern game in which there is too little control — the prevention and treatment of football injuries.

This book has been written to offer teachers, coaches and trainers the opportunity to take greater control of this part of the game and to give them the information which will help them make safe and wise decisions. Too many injuries occur which could have been prevented and too many injuries are incorrectly treated. This book has been written to try to help prevent and treat injuries. It will not, of course, completely remove the need to consult health professionals such as doctors, physiotherapists or chiropodists. We have tried to indicate when such specialist skills are required and when the injury can be managed by the coach and the player without professional help. We believe that it will give coaches the feeling of being in greater control when injuries occur and when players ask how they can prevent injuries and the recurrence of injuries. We hope that it will stimulate interest in this fascinating subject and that readers will try to further their knowledge by attending both a first aid course and an officially organised Football Association course on the treatment of football injuries.

We will be discussing many types of injuries but all can be considered as one of two kinds, depending upon their cause. There are those which result from overuse and those which result from trauma. Injuries resulting from over-use are usually gradual in onset and unrelated to any kind of blow or twist. They are difficult to diagnose and treat and should be left to the professionals such as physiotherapists, doctors and remedial gymnasts in most cases.

Those which result from trauma are, as the phrase indicates, usually of acute onset being caused by a kick or blow or by some sudden movement of the body. The objective of this book is to give basic guidelines on the assessment and management of these traumatic injuries.

## THE CRUCIAL DECISIONS

### Timing
Timing is always important in football. The player with the sense of timing is invaluable. He knows just when to release the ball, when to tackle and when his team mate is going to arrive at the point at which he has laid the ball. Timing is equally important in the management of injuries and in the course of each injury there are three times when crucial decisions have to be made:
   1. 'Should I send him back or substitute him?'— that is the first important decision to be made when a player is injured and on the touchline.
   2. 'Do I need a professional second opinion?' — this is the second important decision. It may have to be made on the touchline or when the team is back in the dressing room after the match. Or it may not even arise until weeks later when an injury which appeared to be a minor injury is not recovering as expected.
   3. 'Is he fit to resume training?' — this is often the most difficult of the three decisions.

### Urgency
All injuries should be treated as quickly, but as calmly, as possible. When it has been decided that a second opinion is required from a doctor, however, it is not always necessary to obtain it quickly. Some cases require medical attention more urgently than others and throughout the book we use the same three terms for the three degrees of urgency:

> *As soon as possible* — when we say medical help should be sought as soon as possible, that means immediately. The player should be taken to hospital while the game is still in progress. If you are going to take a player to hospital ensure that he is given *nothing to eat or drink* in case he needs a general anaesthetic.

*The same day* — when this phrase is used we mean the problem is less urgent. The player should call his general practitioner but, if he is unavailable or unwilling to come to see him — we describe the difficulties of consulting a doctor on page 22 — the player will have to go to hospital. With this type of problem, however, the player may return to his home town before seeking treatment if the injury is sustained when he is playing in an away match.

*Make an appointment to see a doctor* — some injuries should be seen by a doctor but do not need to be seen the same day that the injury occurred. For such injuries it is sufficient for the player to make an appointment with his doctor even though he may have to wait several days before the doctor can see him.

## HOW TO USE THIS BOOK

If you buy a power drill or a motor mower you will be given instructions and we hope that this book will become as useful a tool to you when you are on the touchline as a power drill or motor mower is when you are at home. We therefore suggest that you follow these guidelines when reading and using the book.

Take it with you in your pocket or bag. It is a text book of touchline medicine to be used on the touchline and not kept on the bookshelf. Don't be ashamed to consult it on the touchline or in the dressing room after the match. We do not expect you to carry all the information in your head when you can carry it in your pocket. One piece of advice we warmly recommend to you: when you do consult it while standing or sitting beside an injured player don't do it furtively. Be open about it, involve the player, tell him that you are going to consult a book to see whether or not he needs to see a doctor, make him feel the confidence we hope you will gain from reading this book.

Don't rely on the book alone. It won't make you an expert, although it will tell you how to make the most effective use of the expert help available. Enrol in a first aid course (see page 17) and try to find enough support among your colleagues in other clubs to make it worthwhile for your local Football Association to mount a course on the prevention and treatment of football injuries (see page 23).

## THE GOLDEN RULES

**Play Safe**

In a game it is sometimes necessary to take risks, to throw players forward in an attempt to break a stubborn defence. When managing the injuries of other people there is no scope for taking risks. If you are responsible for a decision affecting the wellbeing of another person you have to be much more cautious than if you were making the same decision about yourself. This applies particularly to those who manage boys' or youths' teams. If a player desperately wants to play you may wish to let him take a risk, but you should let him take the field only after explaining to him, or to his parents if he is a youngster, why you think it is unwise to play. There will be occasions when you should refuse absolutely to let a player take a risk. If a lad is picked for a county boys' team and has a risky ankle on the day of the match, you may decide to let him take the risk and gain a representative honour. If, on the other hand, he wants to play just because he is scared he will lose his place in the team if he doesn't turn out, you should stand firm and tell him that you know his capabilities well enough and that if he plays and breaks down he will definitely lose his place in the team for a couple of months.

Teachers who are responsible for school teams have to be even more cautious than those people running boys' teams in independent clubs. Many parents have a different attitude to injuries when they are sustained in school-time when a teacher is present, and not a few are quick to apply for compensation so that for teachers to play safe is a very important rule. Remember that your decision may have legal as well as medical implications. Don't be too frightened by the legal implications, however. If a teacher acts in the manner in which a parent would reasonably be expected to act no court will hold him responsible but teachers must be more cautious than other coaches, managers or trainers.

Just as you have to be more cautious with players than you would be with yourself we had to be more cautious in the advice we have given than we might be if we were standing beside you on the touchline or in the dressing room. We have followed our own rule — Play Safe.

**Play it Cool**

When your team is under pressure you hope that your players will keep cool while playing as hard and as fast as they can. Keeping cool means that players don't shout angrily and uselessly at one another or stand and clutch their heads when something goes wrong. It means that they don't panic and that they keep thinking and communicating constructively. Often the coolness of a team under pressure flows from one player — a general like Bobby Moore or Franz Beckenbauer — and you must be the source of coolness when a player has been injured. You are the injury general. No matter how worried you are, try not to show it. It makes other people worry and can make the player feel much worse. Research has shown that the amount of pain experienced by hospital patients depends not only on the degree of their injury but also on the confidence they have in those who are helping and this confidence is increased if the helpers appear to know what they are doing.

Be confident, reassure the injured player, tell him confidently that you have a plan of action which will relieve his pain and tell him confidently that the cold sponge will slow down the bleeding in his ankle if that is what you plan to do. Smile, and look confident. Don't smile in such a way that the player thinks you don't appreciate the severity of his injury — to the injured person the injury is always very severe — but give an 'it's going to be all right' smile. Accompany it by putting a blanket round the player's shoulders because a player who is cold or who shivers feels more distress and pain than one who is kept warm. But don't fool yourself. Don't become too confident inwardly but let your outward appearance be calm and reassuring — Play it Cool.

## Look and Listen Before You Touch

One of the most common sights following ankle injury is someone on the touchline grabbing the player's leg in one hand and his foot in the other and waggling it about vigorously to see if the ankle is 'all right'. It is surprising that the foot is not torn off sometimes. Touching the injured part in any way is the last step to take. Before that you should listen to what the player tells you about the way in which the injury happened and where the injured part hurts and you should also be looking for any obvious deformity at the site where the player indicates the pain is greatest. Give the spot the X-ray look. Try to visualise what structure is under the skin and what is happening there as you look. Try to see the blood leaking out from the torn blood vessels. Compare the injured part of the body with the same part on the other side of the player, look at and feel the uninjured ankle or knee so that you learn a little bit about the player's normal anatomy. Only after all this should you consider touching the injured part — Look and Listen Before You Touch.

## Prevention is Better Than Cure

Always think prevention. We appreciate that it is not so dramatic as dealing with gushing blood and a rapidly swelling ankle but it is very important. After every injury ask yourself not only what should be done but what *could have been done* to prevent it and put that lesson into practice in future — Prevention is Better Than Cure.

# 2.
# PRINCIPLES OF TREATMENT

## PSYCHOLOGICAL ASPECTS OF INJURY

As we have already mentioned, psychological factors sometimes influence the way in which a player describes the effects of his injury. We discussed the problem presented by the player who is so keen to play in a certain match that he will not reveal that he is in pain or discomfort. However, this is not the only way in which a player's attitude to his injury influences the manner in which he describes it and consults the coach or trainer.

Some players react dramatically to the slightest knock or twinge, falling down and rolling around, apparently in agony. The reason for this type of reaction may simply be that the player is trying to impress a referee with a bit of histrionics, but there are certain players who react in this way even when there is no possibility of gaining a free kick or penalty and often they react in the same way to a cold in the head, complaining loudly and taking to bed as though they had pneumonia. This type of player usually recovers quickly, especially if you make a fuss of him, for example by using the sponge liberally, reassuring him confidently and giving him a dextrose tablet.

Other players do not respond so dramatically to knocks but worry and brood about every knock and twinge. They are continually bringing minute bruises and cuts to the trainer's attention and keep asking for treatment. The reason for this type of behaviour is that the player is anxious and worried and it is most marked among players to whom the game is very important. The player who worries excessively is not easily reassured, but his anxieties can be allayed if his problem is listened to carefully and the injured part is examined thoroughly before he is told that he is not seriously injured.

These two types of player must be distinguished from the malingerer, the player who magnifies every minor problem and may even invent symptoms if he has none, to avoid training and unattractive matches. The malingerer is usually easy to spot because he is the sort of player who also slacks at training and takes it easy during a match whenever he thinks no-one is watching. He is not so easy to deal with, however, especially when he is a skilful player whose contribution to the team can be great if he makes an effort, because attempts to control him by direct confrontation may make him leave the club. One way to deal with a player who invents an ankle injury to excuse himself from training outside on a cold wet night is to put him to work with weights doing trunk, shoulder and arm exercises until he wishes he were out training with the squad, but the skillful malingerer can usually outwit every trap.

The risk run by the malingerer, and by the type of player who reacts dramatically to injury or the type who worries greatly, is that a serious injury may be missed. The player may have cried wolf so often than insufficient attention is paid to his complaints to detect serious injury. Another type of player runs this risk, the uncomplaining or stoical player. Most teams are fortunate enough to contain a player who always turns up for training, is never late for a match, works hard and unselfishly for ninety minutes and does not blame others or moan when things go wrong. This type of player is often unwilling to complain about minor knocks and he may also keep to himself the fact that he is having the same pain after every match. He will struggle on and aggravate the effects of an injury. This type of person, for he is usually equally uncomplaining at home and at work, may need to be asked directly, 'have you any aches or pains?' after every game if injury is not to be missed.

Finally, remember that the person who is treating injuries also varies in his reaction to injury. Try and be conscious of how anxious you are about a player's injury. You may be too anxious, because the injured player is the son of a close friend for example, and over-react to the injury or you may not be anxious enough because you are worrying about the result of the game and therefore encourage a player to go back when he should really stay off. In both types of situation your judgement will be impaired.

Injury results in damage, but it also causes anxiety in both the person who is injured and the person who is treating him. Both damage and anxiety have to be understood and carefully managed.


## STRUCTURE AND FUNCTION

Throughout this book the emphasis is on the effects of injury on the body's structure; particularly on bones, muscles, tendons and ligaments. However each structure has a function which must always be taken into consideration.

Bones are rigid and support the soft tissue of the body. They form the chassis of the body, which is mobile because bones meet one another at mobile joints. Each joint is enclosed by a capsule of fibrous tissue. This is thickened in certain places where the joint is under greatest strain and these fibrous thickenings are called ligaments. The joints are also stabilized by muscles and tendons as well as by the shape of the bones which meet at the joint.

Tendons are fibrous cords which act as hawsers, running from muscle to bone. A tendon allows a muscle to act at a distance, as a hawser allows an engine to pull on a load many yards away from it. The tendon also allows the line of force of a muscle's action to be charged, as a hawser which runs round a pulley charges the line of force. Roll up your right sleeve and feel how the muscles on the inner aspect of the forearm, the same surface as the palm of the hand, narrow into tendons which are easily visible in front of the wrist. These forearm muscles flex the fingers and flex the hand — observe this on your own hand — and they do this much more effectively and efficiently by narrowing into tendons than they would if the muscles themselves ran across the front of the wrist and the palm of the hand. Flex your wrist towards the forearm as far as it will go and observe how you can still bend your fingers because the tendons slide smoothly round fibrous bands which run under the skin in front of the wrist. These fibrous bands, which lie parallel to the skin creases which you can see, act as a pulley. They change the direction of the tendons and the line of action of the forearm muscles.

Every injury has functional effects and these may be far away from the site at which the structural damage is greatest. If you saw a barn with a roof which was out of line, your first thought would be that something was wrong with the foundations and you would probably be correct. Similarly, a tear in one of the calf muscles which causes the player to limp for several days may lead to pain in the knee joint or the groin on the same limb because they are put under stress by the unbalanced gait. It could also cause pain in the opposite knee and ankle. Sometimes there is little pain at the site of the structural damage which has resulted from an injury and the only effects which are noticed are the secondary functional effects. If the arch of a player's foot begins to fall (see page 68) pain may be felt only in the ankle because the change in the shape of his foot can throw a strain on the ankle joint. In this condition treatment of the ankle will not relieve the pain, only treatment of the fallen arch can do that.

To understand the way in which the body functions it is necessary to appreciate the part played by the nervous system — the brain, spinal cord and nerves. The nerves conduct electrical impulses from the brain and the spinal cord to the muscles. When an electrical impulse arrives at a muscle it stimulates the muscle to contract. However, the nervous system also co-ordinates the functions of the muscles. For example, when a player is knocked off balance by a challenge and lands awkwardly on one leg, electrical impulses stream back from sensors in the muscles, ligaments, tendons and skin of that leg to the spinal cord and brain. The brain calculates the extent and direction of displacement and sends impulses back to the leg muscle to correct the displacement without the player being conscious of what is happening. The reaction is a reflex, and automatic pilots and many other control systems work on the same principle. The muscles which have been stretched contract reflexly and those which have been shortened relax so that the limb becomes vertical again, and a whole series of simultaneous reflexes modify the position of the body, the other leg, the arms, and the player's neck and head so that the player's whole body resumes the vertical position.

## Control of Bleeding

All the structures of the body, bones, ligaments, muscles and tendons for example, are living structures and the function of blood is to keep them alive. Injury to any part of the body results not only in damage to the cells of the tissue which composes that part, such as muscle cells or bone cells; it also results in bleeding because the blood vessels which supply the part which is the site of injury are damaged and torn. The bleeding associated with injuries such as tears of muscles or tendons is very important for three reasons:
1. The leakage of blood can cause further damage to the surrounding cells.
2. The bleeding can cause pain because it causes swelling.
3. The clotting of the blood which has leaked from the torn blood vessels slows down the healing of the tissue which is damaged.
Bleeding may result from damage to a blood vessel of large diameter, that is one which is one or two millimetres in diameter, but it usually results from damage to many hundreds of small blood vessels. Hold your left thumb by pressing the sides of the nail with your right thumb and right index finger. Press and release your left thumb several times and observe the tissue and the nail change colour as dozens of small blood vessels fill and empty. They are too

small to see with the naked eye but if a number are damaged a considerable amount of blood can leak out very quickly. To control bleeding from blood vessels of any size three basic principles must be observed:

1. *Elevation* — let your right hand hang down by your side for five minutes and note how the veins on the back of your hand become distended with blood and how the skin becomes pink as the small blood vessels under the skin fill with blood. Now elevate your hand and hold it above your head observing the veins and the skin colour as you do so. The veins empty and the skin becomes pale as the blood drains out of them. Obviously the elevation of an arm in which an artery was vigorously spurting blood would not stop the bleeding but most bleeding is a gentle ooze from many small blood vessels rather than a spurt from a large artery.

2. *Cold* — take this book to the kitchen and find two bowls which are big enough to contain a hand and wrist. Fill one with very hot water and the other with cold water, preferably with some ice in it. Lay the book down and place one hand in each bowl. Wait for three minutes, then compare the colour of your hands. That which was in the hot water is red because the blood vessels under the skin dilate and fill with blood, as they do when the body is warm as a result of exercise. The hand which was in cold water is white because the blood vessels constrict as a reflex when the skin is cold, which is what happens in cold weather. This reflex response of blood vessels to a change in temperature can be used by trainers and coaches. If the part of the body which has been injured is cooled down the blood vessels which lead to and from the damaged area will constrict and the rate of bleeding will be slowed down.

3. *Pressure* — if you were to come across someone who had been injured in a road traffic accident and who had an open wound in which an artery lay spurting blood, the sensible course of action would be to press down firmly on the artery with your thumb, preferably covered by the cleanest pad you could make. The same principle of direct pressure with a clean pad, preferably a sterile pad (see page 43), is relevant for any type of bleeding from vessels large or small. Tourniquets are never used now because it is known that it is much safer

and more effective to apply pressure directly to the bleeding area. Press down on your thumbnail and see how the area where you press becomes white as blood is pushed out of the blood vessels. The same happens wherever the bleeding is occurring, whether it is in the middle of a muscle, or around a tendon or ligament.

To put the principles into practice is relatively easy. Elevation is obtained by raising the injured part of the body above the heart. Cold is applied to the injured part by means of a pad soaked in cold water, an ice pack (see page 111) or by immersing it in a bucket of cold water. Immersion is very suitable for hand or foot injuries. The use of ice is obviously more effective because ice is a lower temperature than cold water but it has its drawbacks. Care must be taken that the skin is not damaged by ice so it cannot be left on the surface of the skin too long, whereas the cold sponge can be left in contact for a much longer period of time. The easiest way to obtain compression quickly is to apply direct pressure to the area, for example by holding the sponge soaked in cold water to it. For longer periods of time a compression bandage is useful. It is however very difficult to apply a compression bandage (which consists of alternate layers of cotton wool and bandage) properly. Our advice to the person who has not been properly trained in their application is to take a simpler approach. Don't attempt to apply compression bandages to muscle injuries. You can do more harm than good; so rely on cold and elevation. For knee or ankle injuries, however, some form of compression is a useful and relatively safe measure for the first twenty-four hours after the injury. It is not a substitute for cold and elevation however, and should not be taken by the player as an excuse to go to the disco. Wrap a small towel, folded into a six-inch broad strip round the injured part and then bandage it in position, firmly but not tightly, with an elasticated bandage such as the Medisport conforming elastic bandage or the Elastocrepe bandage manufactured by Smith and Nephew Ltd.

### REHABILITATION

The management of football injuries requires two different approaches — treatment and rehabilitation — and both must be carried out simultaneously from the moment of injury. The objective of treatment is to minimise the structural damage of the part which has been injured, primarily by stopping the player from applying further stress to the injured part and by controlling bleeding to help the body's natural healing powers. The objective of rehabilitation is to minimise the effects of injury on other parts of the player's body and to promote the psychological approach and physical exercises which will bring the player back to match fitness as soon as possible.

When a player has injured one part of his body it does not mean that he should rest his whole body. Indeed the opposite is true. He should work the rest of his body as hard as possible so that he maintains his level of fitness. The player who has injured an ankle cannot run but many other types of exercise can be devised which impose demands on muscles in the other parts of his body and which raise his pulse rate sufficiently to maintain his level of heart-lung fitness. Swimming is an excellent rehabilitation exercise, although the leg action of the breast stroke can aggravate a knee injury, and the use of isometric exercises should also be considered.

Even if a player cannot run because of an injury to one knee, the muscles of that leg can still be exercised. For example, the quadriceps muscles which cover the front of the thigh and run to the knee-cap can be exercised isometrically. That is they can be tensed and relaxed without moving the knee joint. Sit down on the floor, put your leg out in front of you and tense your quadriceps muscles with your hand on your knee-cap to feel the effect. Repeat this fifty times and you will appreciate how effective isometric exercises are in making muscles work (see page 88). They are very useful in rehabilitation as they allow the muscles near an injured part to function and to train without working the injured part.

Once a part can be moved without pain it should be brought back to full fitness with a graded series of exercises. For example, the rehabilitation of someone who has suffered a tear to his Achilles tendon (see page 51) should follow this sequence:

1. Full movement of ankle when the player is lying down, that is with no weight on the ankle.
2. Full movement of the ankle when the player is sitting on a chair, with his foot on the ground, that is with only the weight of the leg on the ankle and tendon.
3. Rising up on toes while standing and holding onto a bench or table, that is with slightly less than full weight being borne by the Achilles tendon.
4. Rising onto the toes of both feet.
5. Rising onto the toes of the foot on the side of the injured tendon alone.

6. Standing on a step on the toes of both feet, with the heels unsupported, holding onto some support in front, then allowing the heels to drop as far as possible, and rising on the toes as far as possible.
7. Jogging.
8. Running.
9. Kicking a ball.

Finally, remember the psychological aspects of rehabilitation which have to be worked out for each injured individual. Their psychological reactions to injury which were discussed in the first section of this chapter are relevant here. Each individual reacts differently to injury and to rehabilitation. Some are terrified that they will never play again, some players are frightened that they will lose their place if they are off too long, and some are too lazy to bother about rehabilitation exercises, to mention only three types of reaction which can influence the player's participation in rehabilitation. It is up to the trainer, manager or coach to plan a rehabilitation programme which is best suited to the functional and psychological needs of the individual who has been injured.

In general, it is best for the player to take all the steps in rehabilitation himself. The contribution of the coach or trainer who has not been specifically trained in the management of injury is best restricted to advice and encouragement. If you can call on the services of a trained professional — a doctor, physiotherapist or remedial gymnast — he may use a whole variety of techniques such as ultrasonic treatment or hot and cold treatment. The untrained person can do a little gentle massage — imagine you are bathing a baby not kneading dough — but in our opinion, should only adopt a more vigorous approach under the guidance of a fully trained professional.

## SUPPORTIVE STRAPPING

The principles which we have emphasised in this chapter should all be borne in mind when the subject of supportive strapping is considered. Strapping is a topic on which there are as many opinions as there are on religion. We set out our opinions on the principles of strapping in this chapter because we believe the principles of strapping are more important than the details.

Firstly, the psychological aspects of strapping are as important as the physical aspects of injury. If a player has faith in the strapping on his ankle there is no point in trying to persuade him not to apply it even though years have passed since his injury and he has obviously been fully recovered for many seasons. In fact one of the reasons why we give detailed advice about strapping is so that you will be able to strap someone's ankle or knee safely when he asks you to do it. Sometimes you have to go along with a player's beliefs even though you know that he is fully fit and does not need strapping. Great care has to be used when considering whether or not strapping is necessary for an ankle which has been injured. You should not use strapping to try to convince a player who is nervous about his ankle, knee or muscle that he is fit to play. If he is in doubt he is probably correct and you should not try to bolster his confidence by artificial means.

Secondly, when applying strapping to a joint, it is essential to think of both structure and function. There is a tendency to think of strapping structures which have been damaged as being similar to tying string round a parcel that is likely to fall to bits and to wind round as much tape as possible as tightly as possible to hold the bits of the parcel together. This is not the way to think of strapping. It is more appropriate to think of the strapping as supporting and complementing the function which has been impaired by the structural damage. For example, the objective of ankle strapping is not to apply pressure directly to the ligament which is torn in an attempt to hold the two ends together. The objective is to take the strain off that ligament by applying the tape in such a way that the muscles which normally support the ankle joint and take the strain off that ligament are supported. For this reason we prefer the style of strapping in which the tape is looped under the foot and drawn up like a sling under the foot attaching to the skin on either side of the leg to figure of eight above the ankle strapping (see page 77). The attachment to the skin is, in our opinion, particularly important because it uses the elasticity and the strength of the skin.

Some people become allergic to elastoplast. If they sustain cuts they require the special type of adhesive tape which has been developed for allergic skins. If they require supportive strapping their allergy poses a problem. It is possible to buy gauze or bandage to put under the tape for such players — the Medisport pre-taping underwrap is very good — but the strapping is much less effective because it does not use the skin as part of the system of support. The skin is not just like a piece of wrapping-paper. It is elastic and resists stretching and deformity. Adhesive strapping which attaches directly to the skin and puts it under tension uses these properties of the skin, and complements its normal action. The direct application of strapping to the skin also activates nerve endings in the skin and this results in reflex contraction of the leg muscles in a manner which further supports the ankle.

Strapping can help a player during rehabilitation but it is not a substitute for it. The main resources on which the player must call during the recovery period are the strength of his own muscles and will power and the main source of support will be his coach, trainer or manager, and any other professional who is advising him. Learn how to apply strapping but don't come to rely on it too much.

# 3.
# THE INJURY TEAM

Although this book has been written to help you cope with injuries when you are on your own, there are a number of other people interested in the prevention and treatment of sports injuries — the injury team. It is up to you to build up your own injury team, just as you build up your football team, trying to ensure that you have access to all the necessary skills. Exchange ideas, names and contacts with other trainers and managers.

The members of the injury team are:
1. The British Red Cross Society, The St. John Ambulance Association and Brigade and, in Scotland, The St. Andrew's Ambulance Association.
2. Physiotherapists and Remedial Gymnasts.
3. Chiropodists.
4. Dentists.
5. Osteopaths and Chiropractors.
6. Pharmacists.
7. Doctors — general practitioners and hospital doctors.
8. The Football Association.

In this chapter we are going to describe the skills each have to offer, when use should be made of these specialist skills and how to make contact with someone who can help in each of the groups.

### THE RED CROSS, ST. JOHN AND ST. ANDREW'S

We have not tried to teach you how to do mouth to mouth resuscitation because we believe that it is not possible to do this by words alone. You need a practical demonstration and the opportunity to try the technique using the apparatus which the first aid courses organised by these associations use. We believe everyone should attend a first aid course not just because it complements the knowledge about the management of football injuries which we hope you will acquire from this book but because it includes teaching on other problems, for example burns and scalds, which we believe everyone should know about. These organisations may also be able to help you by the provision of trained first aiders if you are organising a big match or tournament. Contact one of the organisations and find out when you can enroll in a course.

The three organisations have jointly produced an excellent

manual called *First Aid*. It can be purchased from any branch but is best read in conjunction with tuition at a first aid course.


## PHYSIOTHERAPISTS AND REMEDIAL GYMNASTS

For the purpose of the treatment of football injuries these two professions can be regarded as having the same set of skills, although there are important differences between them. Both are skilled in the assessment and treatment of injuries to muscles and joints and both can give excellent advice on prevention.

Most of these professionals work in hospitals although the league clubs all have physiotherapists and remedial gymnasts on their staff. Doctors treat by operation and drugs or by the immobilisation of the affected limb in a plaster but physiotherapists and remedial gymnasts treat injuries by teaching the patient how to use his own body in such a way that the effects of injury are overcome. Sometimes the physiotherapists and remedial gymnast will be involved, and be in charge right from the start of treatment. In other cases, for example where a plaster is necessary to hold a fracture firm, their main contribution comes after the plaster has been taken off and the player has to regain the strength of the muscles which have been weakened as a result of being out of use. They are the key professionals in rehabilitation, in which they may use heat lamps, or ultrasonic waves, or other processing equipment, and they may massage affected muscles but their principal technique is to teach the person how he can best use his muscles to overcome the effects of injury and immobilisation to regain his full potential and reduce the risk of recurrence.

When the injury has been a severe one requiring hospital treatment the player will probably have been seen by a physiotherapist or remedial gymnast but he will not be seen if the injury has been minor. Fortunately most minor injuries heal without the need for this type of professional help but sometimes a muscle or joint injury drags on and breaks down every time the player starts to train or play and this type of situation is one in which physiotherapy or remedial gymnastics can help.

Because most National Health Service physiotherapists and remedial gymnasts work in hospitals it is not possible for a player's general practitioner to arrange for him to be seen by one of them in the same way that he can prescribe drugs and medicines. The general practitioner has to refer the player to a consultant orthopaedic surgeon working in a hospital who can call on the skills of a physiotherapist or remedial gymnast. The general practitioner may say that there is no point in referring the player to hospital because it may be six months or more before people with chronic conditions can be seen. In such a situation a private consultation with a physiotherapist or remedial gymnast should be considered. The general practitioner is unlikely to be upset if this is suggested because he knows, although he will not necessarily admit, that these professionals know more about muscle and joint injuries than he does and because he would probably have called on the services of one had he been able to do so.

To find a physiotherapist or remedial gymnast ask around to see if there is one locally who is specially interested in sports injuries. If this fails look in the Yellow Pages and choose a physiotherapist who has the letters MCSP or SRP after his or her name or a remedial gymnast with the letters MSRG. There is an Association of Chartered Physiotherapists in Sports Medicine (ACPSM), which is a specialist section of the Chartered Society of Physiotherapists. The Chartered Society which is based at 14 Bedford Row, London, WC1R 4ED will link you with the ACPSM which publishes a directory of such physiotherapists in every part of the country. It is not possible to say how much private treatment will cost but you should be given some idea of how many treatments will be required at the first consultation. Also, the physiotherapist may want to contact a doctor about the case so it is wise to inform the player's general practitioner that he is seeking help privately.

## CHIROPODISTS

The chapter on foot problems gives detailed information about the type of problem we believe should be taken to a chiropodist but we take this opportunity to emphasise how important the contribution of the chiropodist can be. If more people consulted qualified chiropodists many of the foot problems which plague older people, and older players, could be prevented and many chronic conditions could be cleared up quickly.

The National Health Service employs chiropodists. Most of their work is with old people but in many parts of the country a chiropody service is available for school children. If a schoolboy has ingrowing toe nails, for example, enquire whether the school health service can offer him a chiropody appointment. (The school secretary will know the address to which you should write). If it is impossible to obtain NHS chiropody or if the waiting time before the chiropodist can see a player is very long a private chiropodist should be consulted. Look in the Yellow Pages and choose a fully qualified State Registered Chiropodist who will have the letters, SR Ch after his name. There is no need to inform the player's general practitioner that this step is being taken.

## DENTISTS

This section should be read in conjunction with the section on mouth injuries (see page 98).

In addition to routine dental care dentists offer two valuable services to football players — the making of mouthguards and the treatment of broken teeth.

There is not the same need for mouthguards in football as in rugby but it is worthwhile for footballers to consider a mouthguard, especially the player who has already lost a tooth or two. The advice of a dentist should be sought but mouthguards cannot be supplied on the National Health Service. They must be purchased privately but are relatively inexpensive when balanced against the loss or permanent damage of a tooth. It is not uncommon for a tooth to be broken when heads clash. If a player is unconscious as the result of a clash of heads which has resulted in damage to his mouth it is important to remember that he may have inhaled a fragment of broken tooth or a whole tooth and he should be turned into the recovery position (see page 96) *as soon as possible.*

It can be difficult to find a dentist on a Saturday or Sunday but there is an emergency dental service in some parts of the country and, if a player has lost a bit of a tooth and is in pain, you should phone the local hospital casualty department and ask if such a scheme is in operation. You can also ask your dentist if he would mind being phoned on a Saturday or Sunday on the rare but serious occasions on which a tooth injury might be sustained. Tell him it should only be about once every two seasons and that you really don't expect him to wait at the end of a phone or to let you know if he is going away, but you would like to know that you could try to contact him. If a dentist, or any other professional, agrees to help you in this way give him a book token or record token at Christmas, as a symbol of your gratitude in addition to his usual professional fees, even if he has never been called upon.

Most hospital casualty departments can call on the services of a dentist who is specially trained in the management of facial injuries. He is not there just to treat people with toothache but, if a player is bleeding profusely and uncontrollably from a tooth socket, or has pain in the bone where the tooth was inserted, or has a painful jaw or cheekbone, he should be taken to the hospital that same day to see the dentist on call even though his teeth are intact. If the player has simply chipped a piece off a tooth you should just give him aspirin or paracetamol (see page 112) and tell him to make an appointment with his own dentist but it can make a difference to the eventual outcome if he receives immediate treatment and you can ask for advice at the casualty department if you cannot contact a dentist directly.

## OSTEOPATHS AND CHIROPRACTORS

There are differences between these two professions but, from the point of view of someone with chronic continuing or recurrent attacks of back pain, they can be regarded as being identical.

The great majority of backaches clear without any specific treatment although they may take a few months to do so. Some problems, however, drag on for many months, or even years, or clear up for no more than a few weeks only to return with equal severity after a seemingly trivial strain. In such cases the player's general practitioner usually refers the affected person to an orthopaedic clinic but in many parts of the country many months have to be passed in pain before a consultant orthopaedic surgeon can be seen. If this is the case or if the surgeon says he can do nothing or an operation is required, the player may then wish to consult an osteopath. Of course a player with a back injury can consult an osteopath or chiropractor without seeing a consultant orthopaedic surgeon, or even his general practitioner, but it is our opinion that is it wise to consult a doctor initially. Remember that some members of the medical profession are still hostile to osteopaths and chiropractors and may react angrily to the sufferer stating that he is thinking of consulting one. Fortunately doctors are beginning to recognise that osteopaths and chiropractors can deal with back and neck problems which conventional medicine is unable to cure and may be able to advise the sufferer whom they should contact.

Make sure that the player chooses a properly qualified professional. In the case of chiropractors look for the letters MBCA after the chiropractor's name and for osteopaths look for the letters MRO or MBNOA or LLCO.

## PHARMACISTS

Pharmacists are the professionals best trained to advise you on the purchase of dressings, antiseptics and other materials necessary for the first aid bag. Not everyone who wears a white coat in a pharmacy is a trained pharmacist so always ask if you can speak to the pharmacist if you have any queries about any of the substances we recommend.

## DOCTORS

Much of this book is concerned with the difficult decisions you have to make about whether to consult a doctor or not. Some problems you can deal with yourself, others should be given medical attention and we hope that you will find that the book helps you to distinguish between the two types of problem. Having decided that a doctor should be consulted you then have a second problem. You have to decide how quickly a doctor needs to see the player. We have classified three degrees of urgency:

1. Very urgent cases which a doctor should see *as soon as possible.*
2. Urgent cases which should be seen by a doctor the same day although the player could, for example, be taken back to his home town if the injury was sustained during an away match.
3. Non–urgent cases which can wait a few days until the doctor can fit the person into his routine surgery schedule. All that needs to be done on the day the injury was sustained or on a Monday if it happens at the weekend is to phone the surgery or health centre for an appointment.

Non–urgent cases should never be taken to a hospital casualty department, or accident and emergency department as it is now called. All very urgent cases such as severe head injuries and suspected fractures should be taken to hospital unless there is a doctor at the ground. The course of action with these two types of problem is clear cut. The handling of urgent cases, however, depends upon the facilities which are available. If your team plays in a small town or village the general practitioner who is on call for the weekend will probably know either you or the player or the club, even if he is not the player's own general practitioner. He may, for example, belong to the same practice as the player's own doctor, if the latter does not happen to be on call. In large cities, however, the situation is often different and a doctor from a deputising service may be on call for a number of practices covering a large area and he may therefore be much less willing to treat such an injury than the doctor in the small town. In large cities, therefore, it may be necessary to take problems to hospital which would be dealt with by a general practitioner in small towns or villages.

Before going to hospital with a problem which is not obviously a hospital case, as a fracture is, it is wise to phone the general practitioner and ask his advice over the phone because the hospital may be reluctant to see the patient unless he has first consulted, and been advised to come by, a general practitioner.

## THE FOOTBALL ASSOCIATION

You can learn a great deal from other coaches, trainers and managers. Use every opportunity you can to exchange information and ideas. Ask your colleagues what they keep in their first aid kits, how they try to prevent blisters, what warming up routine they use, which physiotherapists they have consulted and similar questions. Never underestimate what your colleagues have to teach you, or what you have to teach them, and never overestimate what the experts know. Always keep learning from others.

Much can be learned from such informal meetings. More can be learned if this approach is combined with formal instruction. The three different types of courses which follow the guide lines laid down by the Football Association for School Team Managers, Youth Team Managers and Local Team Managers all include a session on injury management and, of course, ideas about teaching skills and developing fitness, both of which can prevent injuries. Local Associations can also organise courses in the 'basic treatment of injury' which lead to the award of a Football Association Treatment of Injury Certificate. Attendance at such courses should be complemented by attendance at a first aid course organised by the British Red Cross Society, St. John Ambulance Brigade or in Scotland, St. Andrew's Ambulance Brigade.

For those people who have a special interest in this area the Football Association has developed a comprehensive and excellent course followed by examinations which, if passed, lead to the award of the Football Association Certificate in the Treatment and Rehabilitation of Injured Players. This takes three years of study and requires a considerable amount of commitment but, like all such challenges, it can bring greater rewards and creates opportunities for interesting work in many different aspects of the game.

# 4.
# PREVENTION THROUGH TRAINING

## PREVENTION THROUGH SKILL

Training for football or for any other sport is usually considered as a means of improving a player's performance through the development of skills and the improvement of his fitness. However training is also a means of preventing injury.

The development of skills can reduce the risk of injury. Teaching a goalkeeper how to go down correctly at a forward's feet reduces the dangers of head and neck injury — Scottish football has still not recovered from the death of the Celtic goalkeeper John Thomson following a dive at the feet of a young and sporting Rangers centre forward and Bert Trautmann's neck injury has entered football history as a vivid reminder of the dangers of goalkeeping. Teaching a player ball control can allow him to escape a hostile and desperate marker; consider how seldom Stanley Matthews was injured.

It should also be remembered that the development of refereeing skills through proper training can reduce the level of injury not only because a skilful referee can detect and punish dangerous incidents but because a referee who is in control of a game reduces the number of dangerous incidents which take place. Coaching which concentrates on *skills* therefore reduces the risk of injury but there are a number of good books on coaching. We are here primarily concerned with the prevention of injuries by the promotion of *fitness*.

## PREVENTION THROUGH FITNESS

Fitness reduces the probability that a player will be injured and accelerates his rate of recovery in two ways:
1. By its effect on the muscles themselves. Someone with fit muscles is less likely to suffer muscular injuries (see page 47) or ligamentous injuries (see page 72).
2. By increasing general stamina so that a player can participate fully and whole-heartedly for ninety minutes or, if necessary, one hundred and twenty minutes. A player entering whole-heartedly into every encounter is less often injured than one who hangs back or is half-hearted; Kevin Keegan is rarely seriously injured, though few players are more savagely marked.

Fitness has two main aspects: muscular fitness and heart-lung fitness. These are obviously inter-related but they can be considered separately. To demonstrate to a player that there are two aspects of fitness and that each can limit his performance we suggest that he is asked to perform as many pressups as he can, then, after he has recovered, to sprint on the spot for as long as he can. We suggest that the reader lays down the book at this point and performs these two tasks himself.

Both types of exercise can only be sustained for a limited period of time. In the case of the pressups it was muscular fatigue which made you stop, whereas you had to stop sprinting on the spot because of breathlessness. The first is an indicator of muscular fitness, the second of heart-lung fitness, or the lack of it!

## Muscle fitness

Muscles become fitter — that is not only more powerful but capable of sustaining power over a long period of time — if they are made to work. The work which is chosen should be appropriate to the task for which the fitness is required. There is little point in encouraging a football forward to take up weight training unless you can call on someone who is skilled in supervising it. Weight training may develop an impressive looking set of leg muscles but there is no guarantee that they will function any better for the task of playing football. The most appropriate training for muscles is frequent repetition of the type of work for which the training is intended and this obviously differs depending on the players' positions. Every player requires basic stamina, speed and turning ability but each position has its own requirements. For example, strikers need speed over ten yards and shooting power, full backs need to be able to run backwards and turn, midfield men need stamina, and goalkeepers require a comprehensive and special set of muscular abilities (see page 93). This creates obvious difficulties for teams with only one coach or trainer but each club has to achieve some sort of compromise between the specific training needs of each individual player and the resources which it has available for the organisation and supervision of training.

To increase muscle fitness the amount of work required of the muscles must be greater than they can easily perform. This does not necessarily mean that weight training is necessary. What it does mean is that the player must have some measure of his performance which he can use as a standard. If he is working on ten yard sprints a stop watch will be helpful (see page 34); if jumping, some method must be devised to measure the height he can reach and each of these measures must be made over a length of time. If the players are doing repetitive short sprints it is the time of the tenth twenty-yard sprint which is important, or the height of the twentieth jump. Remember, of course, that the fly men save their effort for the time they think you are measuring their performance so don't be too predictable; you may even have to time every sprint or ensure that every jump is above a certain height. However, the measurement of the tenth sprint or the twentieth jump is not only an assessment of muscle fitness. It also involves heart–lung fitness.

## Heart-lung fitness

To understand the importance of heart-lung fitness it is helpful to consider the motor car because there are many similarities between the propulsion of a car by internal combustion and the propulsion of a player by muscular action.

Both require a source of energy. The basic energy source for the car is crude oil, for the player it is food. Oil is refined to produce petrol in refineries but each player is his own refinery. Food is broken down into simple substances in the intestine, absorbed and then converted into the refined energy source — glucose. Petrol and glucose are sources of potential energy. To release that energy the energy source must react with oxygen which is drawn into a car by the air inlets and introduced to the cylinder by the carburettor. In the body the oxygen is drawn into the lungs, it passes into the blood stream and is pumped to the muscle cell by the heart action. In the muscle cells (the body's pistons) oxygen and glucose react when stimulated by a chemical activator, called an enzyme, releasing heat energy and an exhaust gas — carbon dioxide. The enzyme acts like the car's sparking plug. The release of energy results in work — contraction of the muscle fibres or movement of the pistons — and these movements are transformed into propulsion of the body or car by the transmission system, which in the case of the body consists of the muscles, tendons, bones and joints, which enable a footballer to run and kick the ball.

To improve the performance of either car or player it is essential to concentrate on three main factors:

1. The supply of potential energy — in the case of a player it is glucose.
2. The supply of oxygen.
3. The development of power from energy by the muscle fibres.

**CAR**　　　　　　　**FOOTBALLER**

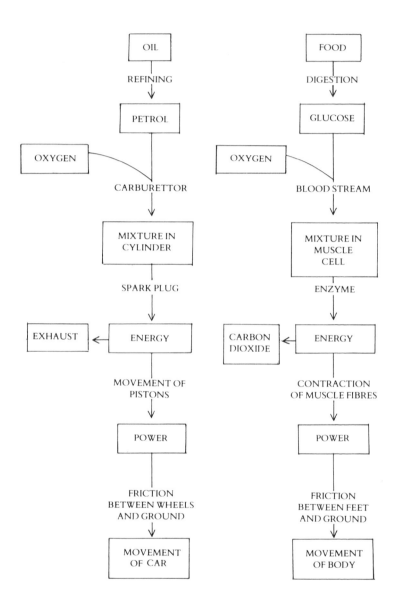

*Glucose supply problems*

Food is a source of energy but, just as it would be not only useless but damaging to put thick black unrefined oil into a car's petrol tank, so the insertion of bits of food, such as tiny particles of steak or toast and marmalade, directly into the muscle cells would result in inflammation and damage, not in the release of energy. Food, like oil, has to be broken down or refined into a simpler substance — glucose — before it can be utilised by the cells of the body. Proteins, fats and complex carbohydrates, such as are found in bread or potatoes, are all partially refined in the intestines before they are absorbed into the body but the process is finished in the liver — the body's petrol tank. In the liver fats, proteins and complex carbohydrates are converted to glucose for immediate use, or for storage as glycogen, which consists of a chain of glucose molecules and is also stored in the muscles themselves.

*Deficiencies.* If the body is unable to supply enough glucose to the muscles they may become weak, or go into cramp (see page 59) but this is not common. Other symptoms of a shortage of glucose are light-headedness, dizziness and general tiredness and some players do develop mild glucose deficiency towards the end of a game. Some people munch glucose or dextrose — a form of purified carbohydrate very like glucose — shortly before kick-off. But it is likely that any beneficial effects of such habits are psychological, due to the player's belief that they will do him good, rather than to any actual effect on the glucose supply to the muscles. It usually takes an hour or so before any of the glucose which is swallowed can be absorbed from the stomach. 'Butterflies' or other symptoms of glucose shortage may also be felt by people who are very anxious or nervous before a game but 'butterflies' and shakiness are due to nervousness not glucose shortage. A light meal rich in carbohydrate taken as part of careful pre-match preparation which is also designed to reassure and calm the anxious player can prevent this type of problem without the need to use glucose or dextrose tablets unless the player fervently believes in their powers (see page 107).

The reasons why a player feels tired after a match are not known with certainty. It may be that his muscle glycogen stores are depleted, but feeding a player with glucose or other forms of carbohydrate, including beer, after a game will not dispel his feeling of tiredness. In a six-a-side tournament some players may be helped by some form of carbohydrate, for example barley sugar between games, but many people feel sick if they try to eat sweets after exercise; so offer sweets to all players but leave it to the individual player to choose whether he wants to accept your offer or not. If a player has to play again in twenty-four hours it is usually possible to motivate him sufficiently to overcome his tiredness but only if he is reasonably fit. Remember that the best preventive measure for post-match tiredness is pre-match fitness. This is partly because fit players are psychologically better prepared for repeated bouts of heavy exercise but it is also because they suffer less from painful stiffness (see page 58). It is more difficult to motivate someone who is tired, stiff and sore than it is to get someone going who is only tired.

Remember also that salt deficiency can cause weakness and cramp if players have been sweating very heavily, for example after four hot evenings of summer training, and table salt on a tomato is a useful antidote after such a heavy session; but extra salt does not need to be taken regularly throughout the season. A deficiency of energy rich carbohydrate, therefore, does not commonly impair a player's performance. A much more common cause of impairment is caused by a surplus of energy.

*Surpluses — A particular problem for coaches, trainers and managers.* If a driver attempts to put more petrol in the car than is needed it will overflow onto his shoes. If a player, or manager or coach, takes in more energy than he requires the surplus is converted into fat. It is easy to assess if you are overweight or obese, to use the medical term. There is no need to consult charts or tables listing 'ideal weights' for different heights. They are as confusing and unhelpful to most people as guides to racing form. All that you or a player has to do is strip off, stand in front of a full length mirror and be honest. Obesity is a problem because it decreases the body's power-to-weight ratio. If a player needs convincing of this, time him over 100 metres then time him again carrying five kilograms of sand in a rucksack.

The cause of obesity is simple; there is a surplus of energy — the amount of energy taken in as food is greater than the amount used in exercise. It is a particular problem in the close season, after injury or after retirement from playing. Energy expenditure decreases in these three situations but many people continue to eat the same amount of food as they did before because their appetite does not always reduce as their energy requirements reduce. In a few lucky people it does, but for most of us our appetite stimulates us to eat much more than we require for the purposes of energy production.

The second complicating factor is that some people need less energy than others to perform the same physical tasks, just as some cars use less petrol than others to cover the same distance. Therefore if two people eat the same amount of food and exercise the same amount one may remain thin while the other, to his annoyance, becomes fat. Why people differ in this way is not known with certainty but some players run to fat more easily than others.

Two steps are essential for a player who has a tendency to run to fat, if he is not to become obese in the close season or after retirement from playing. Firstly, he should keep a careful watch on his weight, weighing himself on the same set of scales at the same time every week — daily weighing is unnecessary. Secondly, he should watch the amount of energy-rich food he takes in. Two types of food are important because they contain large amounts of energy in very small portions of food:– sugary foods and fatty foods. The person who cuts down the amount of exercise he takes should also cut down his intake of these types of food.

## Sugary Foods

| *Obvious sugar* | *Hidden sugar* |
|---|---|
| Granulated sugar, white *and* brown | Beer, including so-called low-calorie lager |
| Sweets | Lemonade and other soft drinks |
| Iced cakes | Cakes |
| Toffee apples | Biscuits |
| Chocolate | |

## Fatty foods

| *Obvious fat* | *Hidden fat* |
|---|---|
| Butter | Lardy cake |
| Cream | Fatty meats |
| Cheese | Sausages |
| | Meat pasties |
| | Nuts |
| | Chips |

This does not mean that the player need go miserably hungry. He can eat as much fruit, wholemeal bread and potatoes as he wants — yes, wholemeal bread and potatoes. Both contain carbohydrate, it is true, but it is not refined carbohydrate, like glucose, and it is at such a

low concentration that a great volume of bread or potatoes has to be
eaten before they result in an energy surplus, provided the potatoes
are not fried in fat or soaked in butter and the bread is not thick with
butter and jam.

*Oxygen supply problems.*
The muscle cells have a very limited store of available energy and
for sustained work such as a game of football a continuous supply of
oxygen is necessary. (A good way to demonstrate this to players is
to light a candle, which is a store of potential energy, and place it
under a large glass jar. Very soon the flame flickers and goes out as
the candle uses up all the oxygen and replaces it by carbon dioxide).
The arrival of oxygen in the muscle cells is the end result of a
number of stages.

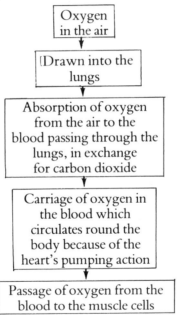

Each of these stages is important, although the first is out of the
control of the coach, who can rarely do anything to alter the amount
of oxygen in the air. International coaches who take teams to play at
high altitudes where less oxygen is available, as in Mexico City,
where the 1970 World Cup was played, have to take this into account
and may have to have oxygen cylinders handy while the players'
bodies are becoming acclimatised to the height.

The second stage, the inspiration of air, results from the combined action of the muscles between the ribs and the diaphragm, which act like bellows and increase the volume of the chest — try it yourself now. During heavy breathing other muscles, particularly those of the neck and shoulders, are also used — watch how players breathe after a session of sprinting. Players who have big chests draw in more air than those with small chests but it is not worth directing special attention to chest expansion as a training objective. The musculature of the chest will develop if the measures we suggest for improvement of the whole oxygen supply system are adopted.

Lung tissue is very like an ordinary bathroom sponge with air in the spaces and a whole network of very small blood vessels in the solid material. Oxygen from the air passes across a very thin layer of tissue to enter the blood, while carbon dioxide passes the other way from the blood to the air spaces of the lung. Training of the sort we will describe increases the lungs' ability to handle oxygen and carbon dioxide. The precise mechanisms by which this happens are unknown but it seems likely that the number of blood vessels in the lungs increases.

One other factor must be mentioned because it can have a significant effect on lung function — cigarette smoking. Much publicity has been given to the serious effect of cigarettes — lung cancer, heart disease and bronchitis — but regular smoking has other effects which are less serious than these diseases but which impair the lungs' capacity to absorb oxygen. Even in teenagers it is possible to show the effects of cigarettes on lungs' function. This point is worth emphasising particularly for those who run boys' and youths' teams. We do so partly because mild effects in a young smoker can become serious as he grows older but also because the managers and coaches of such teams are often looked up to by their players in a way which those who run senior teams are not. If a person responsible for a boys' team does not smoke when he is with them, even if he smokes on other occasions, he sets an example which may encourage his lads either not to start smoking, resisting the hard-man image of the smoker, and may persuade others to stop, or try to stop. It is not easy to stop smoking but it can be done and the encouragement of his manager or coach may help a boy to do so. Useful advice for someone who wants to stop smoking, or for a person trying to help, is contained in the Health Education Council booklet, *The Smoker's Guide to Non-Smoking*, which should be available free from your health centre or doctor's surgery. (If the receptionist doesn't know of the booklet's existence or whereabouts, ask if you can speak to the health visitor).

Training can also help the next stage in the oxygen supply system — the transport of oxygen by the blood to the cells where it is needed because it can strengthen the heart. The heart of a fit person can pump larger volumes of blood round the circulation than the heart of someone who is not so fit can pump in the same period of time. This obviously increases the amount of oxygen carried to the muscles because larger volumes of blood carry larger volumes of oxygen.

*Improving the muscle cells.* Recent research suggests that the passage of oxygen from the blood to the muscle cells also increases as the player becomes fitter. The muscle cells of a fit person are able to extract more oxygen from the blood which flows past them than the muscle cells of someone who is less fit. This is not just because they are bigger or are working harder. The cells actually become more efficient at drawing in oxygen. This piece of research increases the importance of individually tailoring the training of each player to ensure that the muscles he uses most in training are those he will use most in a match.

*Training in principle and practice*
*The loading principle.* A number of different methods — such as circuit training, sprints and distance running, can bring about an increase in the body's capacity for supplying oxygen to the muscle cells, provided that one basic principle is observed. That principle is the *loading principle*. The player must work at a rate which is beyond the comfort level, applying a load to his oxygen supply system which is greater than it can cope with easily. The result of loading the oxygen supply system is that it increases its capacity until it can deal with this level of loading easily. At this stage, a new, greater load must be applied. In other words it is useless doing long hours of gentle exercise. What is required is short periods, for the players cannot take more than short periods, of heavy exercise and the best way to measure the heaviness of the exercise is to use the players own pulse or to use a stop watch.

*Pulse counting and stopwatching.* The pulse is easily found — particularly after exercise — either in front of the wrist running beside the main central tendon on the same side as the thumb or in the neck below the angle of the jaw or just in front of the ear.

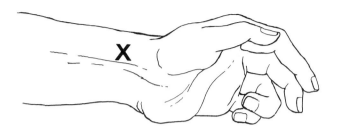

Fig. 1  X marks the spot where the pulse is most easily felt.

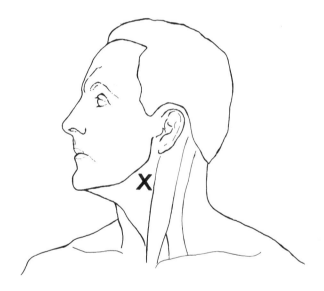

Fig. 2  X marks the spot where the pulse is most easily felt.

Take your pulse now, take it over a period of one minute. If you have been sitting reading this book for ten minutes or longer you can take this to be your Resting Pulse Rate. In general the fitter the person the lower his resting pulse rate will be, not because fit people require less oxygen when they are sitting still but because the big heart of a fit person doesn't need to pump as fast. Now lay the book down and, provided that you are reasonably fit and can take heavy exercise, run on the spot as hard as you can for one minute. Then count your pulse rate, over thirty seconds this time, immediately you have finished. Record this, wait thirty seconds longer and then count it for the first thirty seconds of every minute until it returns to the Resting Pulse Rate. The reason that the pulse does not drop to the resting rate immediately after exercise stops is that some energy stores are used up early in exercise, before the supply of oxygen has time to increase, and these depleted stores must be replenished after the exercise stops.

In general, the fitter someone is the less his pulse will rise during exercise and the quicker it will come back to the resting rate. Fit people are less disturbed by exercise than those who are not so fit. However, many factors affect the rise in pulse rate during exercise, a rise stimulated mainly by the decrease in oxygen and increase in carbon dioxide for the blood; so pulse rates cannot be used to compare one player with another. If one player's pulse rises to 140 beats per minute after training while that of another rises to no more than 110 beats per minute it cannot be concluded that the one with a lower pulse rate is twenty per cent fitter. He might, to give only two possibilities, have been working twenty per cent less hard or have been ten per cent fitter and working thirty per cent less. Although the pulse rate cannot be used to compare one player with another it is very useful in allowing a player to compare himself with himself, that is to compare himself at rest with himself while working, and it is possible to calculate a pulse rate at which to aim to satisfy the loading principle.

The pulse rate which has to be achieved if training is to achieve an improvement in the function of the oxygen supply system — the Loading Pulse Rate — can be calculated from the following formula which should only be used by fit players.

Necessary increase required equals: $\frac{3}{5}$ (220 minus player's age in years minus his Resting Pulse Rate)

If, for example, I am a 35 year-old player with a Resting Pulse Rate of 60 beats per minute I have to increase my pulse rate by:

$$\frac{3}{5}(220-35-60)$$

$$\frac{3}{5} \times 125$$

$$3 \times 25$$

$$= 75 \text{ beats per minute.}$$

Therefore I must aim for a pulse rate of 135 to be maintained for at least fifteen minutes per session. This is the Loading Pulse Rate.

Using this principle a player needs no equipment to train other than a watch with a second hand. He can train as well in a prison cell, as many people have, or in a hotel bedroom as in a gym or in a field. Pulse counting cannot completely overcome the major problem faced by trainers — boredom — but it can help, as it gives a player his own goal to which he can work each training session. It is the task of the trainer to design training methods, incorporating a competitive element and work in teams, but tailored to the personalities of the players in his squad to prevent boredom. Pulse counting cannot help with the other major headache for trainers, the lazy player. Someone who is lazy because he lacks motivation may say he is reaching and maintaining the necessary pulse rate although he is well below it. The trainer can of course take the pulse of such a player himself but a better approach is to use a stopwatch.

The purchase of a stopwatch gives the trainer a very useful tool for training the whole squad not just for assessing the performances of players he suspects of slacking. If a player likes distance running, for example cross country running, the use of a stopwatch allows the player to set targets for improvement with a precision which is not possible with pulse counting. For example, suppose a player enjoys a run over a particular hilly route taking about twelve minutes with his pulse raised to the necessary rate. It is difficult for him to measure an increase in pulse rate, say from 140 to 142 beats per minute as he attempts to improve his performance and increase the load. It is however possible to chart the decrease in his time from twelve minutes twenty-four seconds to twelve minutes eighteen then to twelve minutes eleven seconds with great precision using a stopwatch. Stopwatching is also useful in allowing the player to measure his increase in fitness over a long period of time, say over a two month period.

## FITNESS TRAINING FOR BOYS

Now and again one sees a squad of boys earnestly doing circuit training or sprints. In our opinion this is completely unnecessary and may do some harm as it may bore the boys so much that they give up football. Football is a game to be enjoyed at all ages. Older players have to be kept fit through training to enjoy the game fully but boys run about so much that they do not need special fitness training. The emphasis should be on skills until they reach the early teens and discover there are other things to chase than footballs: then they need training as well as coaching. Remember, however, that sprinting is a skill which can be taught. Some people are naturally better sprinters than others but the speed of every player, young and old, can be increased if they are coached by someone who understands the theory of sprinting. Too often players and coaches assume that speed will increase if spikes are used for training. This is not the case but it is worthwhile linking up with a local athletic club and encouraging players to join and run for the club so that they can receive the benefit of good coaching in sprinting.

# 5.
# SKIN WOUNDS

Attendance at a first aid course run by the Red Cross, St. John's or St. Andrew's Ambulance Association is particularly helpful in learning the principles and practice of managing skin injuries.

## PREVENTION OF SKIN INJURIES

### Accidents?

The term accident implies that the event which took place was the end result of a chain of events which was completely out of the control of the individual involved. It is implied and often stated that the event was the result of 'fate', or 'bad luck'. Children, and some adults, state that 'it broke' or 'it fell' when a plate falls to the ground. That is the way they talk about an accident. They prefer to describe what happened in this way rather than make the longer and more accurate statement 'I did not put the plate on the table properly and the weight of the part which was over the edge caused the plate to tilt above the edge of the table and fall'. A more accurate definition of an accident, therefore, would be that it is the end result of a chain of events which was either not foreseen when the earlier events were taking place or that it is a result which was foreseen but was thought to be so unlikely that it was unnecessary to take steps to avoid it. For example, a cut on the shin bone of a player not wearing shin guards is not caused by 'fate' or 'bad luck'. It is the result of the player either not considering the possibility of a boot on the shin or, having considered the possibility that he might be kicked, deciding that it was so unlikely to happen — 'it won't happen to me' — that he left his shin guards in his bag instead of putting them on.

Accidents are preventable, not all of them it is true, but enough of them to make the word prevention a very important one in the vocabulary of the trainer, manager, coach and player.

### Protecting the shin and ankle

Cuts over the shin bone can be very troublesome but many can be prevented if shin guards are worn. Unfortunately some young players have adapted the habit of wearing their socks rolled right down over their ankles leaving their legs unprotected. A very small number are probably seriously annoyed by wearing their socks up but they are only a minority; the rest are followers of fashion who do not appreciate that the few top class players who wear their socks like this are much more skilful and better able to avoid trouble than they are. (Some players believe that their tie-ups cause cramp but cramp should not be a problem if the player is fit and if the tie-ups are not too tight). With a boys' team or youths' team it is possible to take a hard line and lay down a simple rule: no shin guards, no game. However those people who manage teams of adults do not have this degree of authority and must use persuasion.

Cuts around the ankle are uncommon but can be serious. They can be prevented either by taping cotton wool padding around the ankle bones or, more simply and cheaply, by wearing an extra pair of socks with the feet cut off rolled down over the ankle.

## Prevention of abrasions

An abrasion or 'grass burn' is the type of injury sustained by a fall on hard ground, blaize, shale or ash pitches. The skin is scraped off and blood seeps through from the tissue underneath, just as metal is exposed when paint is rubbed off a car by a brick wall. Players can reduce the risk of such injuries by wearing knee bandages or tracksuit trousers. This is very important for goalkeepers and, fortunately, First Division goalkeepers are setting a good example but *all* players in boys' teams should be instructed to wear tracksuit trousers when conditions are such that abrasions are likely. Goalkeepers will benefit from applying a thick layer of vaseline to the side of the hips and thighs, the areas at high risk, inside their shorts or tracksuit trousers. If the abrasion is in an exposed position, on the side of the thigh just above the knee for example, and requires a greater degree of protection, then vaseline can provide a dressing which will not stick to the raw surface (see page 110).

Long sleeved shirts prevent abrasions on the elbows and forearms but there may be resistance to the wearing of gloves, especially among adults. It is, however, worthwhile pointing out to players the protection which gloves can offer to those whose livelihood depends on their hands, for example draughtsmen or turners; a serious abrasion can put a hand, and therefore its owner, out of work for several weeks.

Remember that most players are more nervous on hard grounds, although many would never admit it, and a player protected against abrasion will be a more confident, committed and effective player.

## Groundsmen and Referees

They have a contribution to make. In many public parks with grass playing surfaces it is possible to move the goal areas fifteen yards either to the side or forwards/backwards. This provides a safer surface for goalkeepers at the start of the season than the baked earth area with no more than a few brave new grass shoots peeping through which often greets the goalie after a dry summer. Referees can prevent cuts, not only by preventing and controlling dangerous play but by checking players' boots. Studs can develop sharp edges, especially where the players have to walk over hard surfaces from the changing room to the pitch.

PRINCIPLES OF TREATMENT

## Cleaning and disinfection

Whenever the skin is broken the wound must be carefully cleaned *and disinfected*. The term 'dirty' is often used to describe wounds by doctors as well as by people who are not medically qualified. However the word 'dirty' is not very precise and it is important to define the word more accurately. When doctors act to clear a wound of dirt they are concerned about two distinct problems: the presence of particles in the wound and the presence of bacteria.

The presence of particles — dust, grit, earth, or blaize — interferes with normal wound healing and can cause a permanent discoloured scar like a tattoo, which would not have developed if the wound had been cleansed of particles immediately after it had been sustained. To clean a wound of particles all that is required is running water, soap and, if the player can take it, a nailbrush.

The rapid multiplication of bacteria — sometimes called germs — can lead to a wound infection which can slow down the healing process. Most bacteria will also be cleared from a wound with the use of soap, water and nailbrush but some will remain in the wound because they are much smaller than dust particles. A different approach is therefore needed to clear the wound of bacteria because of their smaller size and because bacteria can migrate to the wound from the surrounding skin even though it looks clean and has been recently washed with soap and water. (Bacteria are always present on the skin, except after a surgeon or nurse has spent ten minutes scrubbing before an operation). To kill any bacteria left after the initial washing and to deal with any which migrate into the wound while it is healing an antiseptic is required. The best antiseptic is *Hydrogen Peroxide Solution* which must be stored in a *tightly stopped* bottle and diluted with an equal volume of water before it is applied

to the wound. Pour the hydrogen peroxide on the wound — DO
NOT LET IT ENTER THE EYES IF THE WOUND IS ON
THE FACE OR SCALP — and observe the satisfying froth caused
by the chemical reaction which takes place as it disinfects the
wound. After initial disinfection the wound should be kept clean
and exposed to the air as much as possible, being covered only to
stop it bleeding or being irritated by clothing or when there is a risk
that dirt will re-enter the healing wound, at work for instance.
There is no need to use hydrogen peroxide again after the disinfection immediately following the injury. If an infection develops
later on an antibiotic may be required.

All wounds look a little red round the margins while they are
healing. This is due to the increased blood supply to the area which
conveys oxygen and nutrients to the healing tissues. That is normal.
If an infection is developing due to the multiplication of bacteria in
the wound the area surrounding the wound will become: (a) very
red over a large and expanding area; (b) swollen; (c) painful; (d)
warm. These signs are not evident until about twenty-four hours
after a wound, so it is a wise practice to visit any player about whose
wound you are worried twenty-four hours after you have carried out
the initial disinfection. If the infection is left untreated, pus will
gather in the wound. Lymph glands in the groin, if the wound is
on the lower limb, or in the armpit, if it is on the upper limb, will
become swollen and tender. The player may also feel generally
unwell and have a fever. If you suspect that infection is developing,
a doctor should be consulted that same day because the sooner
antibiotic treatment is started the better.

Antiseptics are chemicals which kill bacteria but they only act on
the surface of the wound. Antibiotics are also chemicals which kill
bacteria but they can be taken by mouth or given by injection and
spread throughout all the tissues, killing the bacteria wherever they
are in the body. If antibiotics are prescribed it is essential that they
are taken *exactly as the doctor instructed*. Even though the player feels
better after two days he should continue taking them for five days if
that was the length of time the doctor said he should continue,
unless of course the antibiotics are making him feel unwell. Antibiotics are very beneficial but they occasionally cause unpleasant
symptoms, called side-effects by doctors. The common side-effects
are sickness and diarrhoea but skin rashes and other problems also
sometimes develop. If the player develops any new symptoms after
he has started to take antibiotics he should consult the doctor who
prescribed them or the pharmacist who supplied them the same
day.

It is appropriate at this point to define the other term frequently used when discussing wounds — sterile. A sterile dressing does not kill bacteria but it has been treated in such a way that you can be confident that it contains no bacteria and therefore cannot introduce any infection to the wound. The trainer's bag should contain both sterile *and* antiseptic dressings (see page 110), and these can be bought at a pharmacy, but antibiotics have to be obtained from a doctor. He prescribes them according to the needs of the individual who has an infection.

## Tetanus

One type of infection merits special mention — tetanus or lockjaw. Tetanus is a rare but very serious bacterial infection. It can arise from a mere scratch and it does not cause redness, swelling, warmth or tenderness at the site of the wound like other infections. Instead the bacterial poison, which is called a toxin, spreads to the brain where it causes paralysis and the infection can be fatal. It can, however, be prevented by the injection of inactivated and safe bacterial toxin called Tetanus Toxoid. Babies have three doses, then children have 'booster' doses at five and fifteen at school. After leaving school it is up to the individual to ensure that he has a booster dose every ten years.

MAKE SURE ALL YOUR PLAYERS HAVE HAD AN IN-JECTION AT THE AGE OF FIVE IF THEY ARE UNDER FIFTEEN, AND AT FIFTEEN IF THEY ARE UNDER TWENTY FIVE. MAKE SURE THAT OLDER PLAYERS HAVE HAD A BOOSTER WITHIN THE LAST TEN YEARS.

If a player has not had the necessary injections, or is unsure if he has had them or not, he should make an appointment at his general practitioner's surgery or at the clinic at work, if his work place is big enough to have one.

Although the ten year rule is used for the timing of booster injections, a player who has a very dirty wound or one which is difficult to clean should have a booster if he has not had one in the last five years.

PRACTICAL TREATMENT

## Cuts

Cuts are linear wounds, which can be caused by sharp objects such as broken glass or by 'bursting' trauma such as a clash of heads.

Because skin is elastic cuts often gape open and blood flows from blood vessels in the skin. Most cuts only affect the superficial layers of the skin. Some deeper cuts, however, damage underlying structures and must be treated by a doctor. Take the player to hospital if you cannot get him quickly seen by a doctor if any of these symptoms are present:

1. If there is numbness or tingling or loss of power in the limb on which the cut is situated, a nerve may have been affected.
2. If there is inability to move a joint or a deformity of a joint in the part of the limb peripheral to the cut, e.g. in the hand if the cut is on the wrist, a tendon may be involved.
3. If there is blood pumping from the wound an artery may be involved.
4. If you think there may still be some object in the wound after you have cleaned it.

The first aid treatment of bleeding is the same whether the blood is flowing slowly and gently, or pumping:

1. Remove any obvious foreign body, such as a splinter of wood, from the wound with a pair of tweezers but do not poke about in it.
2. Press a sterile pad to the wound and hold it there firmly.
3. If the cut is on a limb elevate the part of the body so that it is as far above the level of the heart as possible. This allows the force of gravity to empty the blood vessels. Observe this by letting your hand hang down so that the veins fill with blood. Then lift it slowly, and watch the veins closely and see how they empty as the hand is lifted above the level of the heart. You may have to lie the person down to achieve this if the cut is on the leg.
4. Press firmly but not painfully on the cut and on the skin surrounding it. You may have to apply pressure for thirty minutes or more but the cut will stop bleeding using this technique. (It is now realised that the tourniquet is useless and dangerous and should *never* be used).
5. When bleeding has stopped see if you can press the edges of the cut together. If you cannot do this, or if yellow fat bulges out of the cut, stitches may be required and you should take the player to a doctor *as soon as possible*. If the edges can be brought together use 'Butterfly strips' (see page 111) to hold them together. A spray which applies a film is also useful. It seals the area, preventing bacterial immigration, and holds the edges of the cut together, but allows the skin to breathe.

Leave the wound open to the air whenever possible. If it has to be covered, use an adhesive plaster if the cut is small. Use a sterilised wound dressing if it is too large for a plaster but encourage the player to remove the plaster as often as possible to let the air at the wound. A sterile pad of lint or gauze is satisfactory if the wound is to be seen by a doctor within a few hours but, if you wish to apply a dressing to stay on for a day or longer, use a prepared dressing which will not stick to the wound (see page 110).

## Puncture wounds

Puncture wounds are caused by nails or drawing pins, or slivers of glass. They are dangerous because the wound is often deep, although it looks small and innocent, and bacteria may have been driven deep into the tissues. If the puncture wound was caused by a clean drawing pin lying on a clean gymnasium floor treat the wound with hydrogen peroxide solution mixed with equal volume of water and do not put a dressing on it unless it is bleeding, in which case a dressing should be applied only until the bleeding has stopped. If the nail on the ground was dirty, the player should be seen by a doctor the same day and must be taken to hospital if a doctor cannot be consulted any other way (see page 22). The wound may need to be explored and the player will require a tetanus booster if he has not had one in the recent past (see page 43).

## Abrasion

An abrasion, is the result of the skin being scraped along a harder substance, usually the ground. The superficial layers of the skin are rubbed off by the friction. Abrasions should be cleaned and disinfected thoroughly but this can be difficult as many 'raw' nerves are exposed as a result of an abrasion and the surface may be painful, whereas in a cut or puncture wound very few nerves are involved. If you can see particles of dirt in an abrasion after you have tried to clean the wound the player should see a doctor that same day. THIS RULE IS VITALLY IMPORTANT IF THE ABRASION IS ON THE FACE OR IF A BOY OR YOUTH IS AFFECTED. An inadequately cleaned abrasion can result in an unsightly scar and it may be necessary to give the player a general anaesthetic to allow the wound to be scrubbed.

Once the abrasion has been cleaned nature does the rest. A scab or crust forms over the surface and provides an excellent dressing which should be left alone until it falls off. While the scab is forming the abrasion should be left open to the air if possible. If this is impossible, for example if the skin over the hip bone has been rubbed off, an antiseptic dressing must be used but every opportunity possible should be taken to expose the site to the air.

If a player wishes to play with a healing abrasion it can be protected by applying a thick layer of vaseline or by a non-adhesive dressing (see page 110).

# 6.
# MUSCLES AND TENDONS

A muscle joins two bones on either side of a joint. The calf muscles, for example, are attached to the back of the leg bones, below the knee, and to the bones of the foot at the heel by the Achilles tendon. A tendon is a thin, strong cord or sheet of fibrous tissue which acts like a hawser joining a winch, the muscle, to a distant object which is to be moved — a bone. The fibrous tissue which makes up the tendon does not contract, like muscle tissue does, although it does stretch a little when it is pulled taut, as a rope stretches when it takes strain.

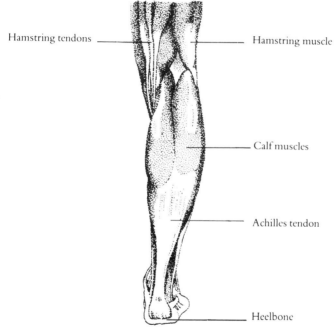

Hamstring tendons _____                    _____ Hamstring muscle

_____ Calf muscles

_____ Achilles tendon

_____ Heelbone

Fig. 3 View of the right calf from the rear with the skin removed to show the calf muscles blending into the Achilles tendon which joins the muscle to the heel bone. Note also the hamstring tendon joining the calf muscle.

Take a piece of meat from the fridge and examine it, get the feel of it. A piece of meat on a bone, a leg of lamb for example, demonstrates the anatomy of muscle clearly. The red meat, the muscle tissue, is obvious. Surrounding it is a white shiny cover of fibrous tissue and sheets of the same substance run from the surface to the bone dividing and sub-dividing the meat into many sections. The muscle you can see and feel in your calf is made up of very small fibres which are grouped together in bundles, like the strands of meat you can see when you cut a steak. The fibres do not run the whole length of the muscle. Those at the end are joined directly to bone — observe the attachment of muscle fibres to bone in the leg of lamb. Those in the inside bind in with other muscle fibres at both ends and the remainder are attached to the sheets of fibrous tissue which surround muscles and run through it. Near the end of a muscle fibres may bind into the fibrous tissue of a tendon — observe the tendon on the leg of lamb. (Ligaments are of similar structure to tendons but they have nothing to do with muscles. They attach bones to bones and act as joint stabilisers — see page 72).

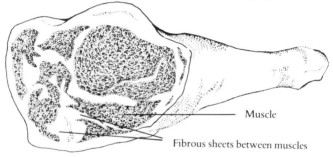

Muscle

Fibrous sheets between muscles

Fig. 4 Cross-section of a leg of lamb showing the sheets of fibrous tissue to which muscle fibres are attached.

When a muscle contracts, all the fibres in it contract in a co-ordinated manner and the two bones at either end are brought closer together; in the case of the calf muscles the foot is tilted downwards, pivoting round the ankle joint and the heel moves closer to the leg bone.

If the contraction is very rapid or if the muscle is stretched suddenly some muscle fibres may be torn loose from their attachments to bone or to the sheets of fibrous tissue; these may also be torn from their attachment to the tendon or the tendon itself may be torn.

## Muscle Injuries; Tears, Pulls and Strains

These terms all describe the same sort of injury and there are no clearcut differences between them. The basic injury is that some of the small muscle fibres are torn away from their attachment to tendon, or bone or to other muscle fibres. The muscle is made up of a great number of small fibres which lie embedded in connective tissue. The shortening of the muscles which takes place during contraction is brought about by the shortening of each of the muscle fibres and the lengthening during relaxation takes place similarly by a relaxation of all the fibres which make up the muscle. This means that each of the fibres has to relax when the muscle is stretched and they may have to do this very quickly when the muscle is stretched violently. If the fibres do not relax quickly enough the harness of connective tissue is torn and the blood vessels which run in the connective tissue may also be torn. This is the cause of a pulled muscle. The quadriceps is, in fact, seldom torn, because it is not often stretched very rapidly and because most players have quadriceps which are very fit. Kicking a football and running develops the quadriceps and therefore footballers have quadriceps muscles which are kept in a state of fitness, able to relax and contract, that is to lengthen and shorten, quickly and smoothly. In many players, however, the hamstring muscles at the back of the thigh, running from the back of the pelvis, under the buttock muscles, to the back of the leg bones below the knee (see page 55) are much less well developed and less fit. Because they are frequently stretched very rapidly and violently during the act of kicking a ball, the hamstrings are particularly prone to pulls.

The first point to make about pulled muscles is that they are preventable and the two methods of prevention are: first, a high degree of muscle fitness (see page 26) and secondly, adequate warming up (see page 51).

If a player does pull a muscle during a game or training he should not continue playing and steps should be taken to stop the bleeding which occurs when the fibres are torn apart. The steps are therefore the same as those advised for treating a dead leg (see page 61).

1. The immediate elevation of the affected muscle above the level of the heart.
2. The application of an ice-bag (see page 111).
3. The application of gentle pressure, such as that necessary to hold the ice-bag in place. For the journey home tie a bandage round the muscle firmly but not tightly.

The player should then rest for twenty-four hours with the part elevated.

Deciding when a player should return to train and then to play after pulling a muscle is one of the most difficult of all decisions in the treatment of football injuries. If the player has damaged a ligament, in his ankle for example, the disappearance of pain and swelling are fairly safe indicators that he can commence gentle training but most people have had the experience of starting training again after pulling a muscle with the feeling that the muscle has fully recovered only to be disappointed by a sudden recurrence of the injury as soon as it is stretched. The important principles to observe are that training must be started *very* gently and that the time devoted to loosening off the muscle fibres before training must be increased. We suggest that, instead of the exercises in the section on loosening up (see page 51) being performed only once they should be repeated five times, with two minutes walking between each set.

## Strapping

Many players rely on elastoplast strapping to support a pulled muscle. Strapping has a part to play but, in our experience, only a small part, less than the contribution which ankle strapping can make to ankle recovery from a ligament injury. The reason for this is it is much more difficult to apply strapping to a muscle in a way which supports the damaged tissues than it is to lay it on parallel to the fibres of the damaged ankle ligaments (see page 00).

The principle of strapping muscles is that the elastoplast should follow the direction of the tissue it is meant to be supporting — connective tissue fibres in ligaments and tendons or muscle fibres. There is no point in trying to strap a muscle if it is still painful. If there is pain the player is not fit to play. If you are in any doubt about the player's fitness to play, you should not rely on strapping to compensate for the healing which has not taken place and you should advise the player not to play.

If applied by someone who does not really have the skill, strapping can be useless. Even worse it can lead to further injury by creating a false sense of security. The only really effective means of supporting muscles which have been pulled is by helping them become as fit as possible and by ensuring that they are properly loosened off during warming up before every training session or game.

### ACHILLES TENDON INJURIES

The Achilles tendon runs from the calf muscles to the heel bone. Put your hand down and feel it now. While remaining seated contract the calf muscles and lift your heel off the ground to feel it work. Now put the heel back on the ground and feel how the calf muscles and Achilles tendon are stretched. Now move your foot forward, stretch your leg out in front of you a little but keep it flat on the ground and feel how the strain is taken off the calf muscles and the tendon.

The Achilles tendon can tear completely across. If it does the diagnosis is usually clear. The player collapses in severe pain and is unable to rise. He may say that he has been kicked on the back of the leg, but as this is reported by people who rupture their Achilles tendon while playing squash or running between the wickets the sensation of being kicked does not necessarily mean that the player has been kicked. The player should be given *nothing to eat or drink* and should be taken to hospital *as soon as possible*. Minor tears of the tendon are not uncommon. They can occur anywhere along its length, at the lower end near the heel, when they have to be distinguished from other causes of pain around the heel (see page 69), in the middle, or at the upper end where the tendon and calf muscles blend into one another. The initial management is the same as for other ankle injuries — elevation, cold and pressure. Care is needed during the period of recovery and we have already described a series of rehabilitation exercises (see page 12).

Strapping of the Achilles tendon is difficult but can be done if cotton wool is used to pad the ankle and is supported by horizontal pieces of elastoplast running round to the front of the ankle.

## THE PREVENTION OF MUSCLE INJURIES

The first, and most important, means of preventing injury to muscles, is the promotion of general muscular fitness, a subject we have already discussed(see page 26). The preparation of the muscles immediately before a match, what is usually referred to as 'warming up' is also of vital importance.

A newcomer to a team of experienced players nervously put on his kit for his first match. In his haste he was the first to be ready and sat nervously drumming his burnished boots on the dressing room floor while the rest of the team donned kit that was grubbier. Eventually all were changed and the captain shouted, 'Right lads, warm up'. The new boy jumped up, turned to face the wall and began doing energetic step-ups until he eventually became aware (although he was staring at the wall immediately in front of him) that no one else was joining in. He looked round and saw the rest of the team jostling for position in front of the small two-bar electric fire which heated the dressing room!

Everyone has his own definition of warming up and players differ very much in their attitudes towards it. These individual differences must be respected (as we will emphasise) but the main objectives can be considered under three general headings:

1. Warming up — increasing the blood flow to the skin. This makes players feel better.
2. Loosening up — preparing the muscle fibres for action. This reduces the risk of muscle injury.
3. Steaming up — building up team spirit. This overcomes the effect of pre-match nerves.

## Warming up

Normally the skin is at a lower temperature than the rest of the body because many of the blood vessels which run below the surface of the skin are contracted. To prevent the body overheating as a result of exercise these blood vessels open up, the skin becomes flushed and the individual feels warm because the heat-sensing nerve endings in the skin are warmed up, just as they are by the sun. The flow of blood through the skin is like the flow of water through a car's radiator. Any type of exercise gives this sensation of warmth and it is important to try to achieve this in the dressing room on cold or wet days. If a player runs out into wind and rain, or both, feeling cold he will probably stay cold especially if he is in a position in which he has not much running to do, in goal for example. A cold player is a miserable player and miserable players rarely reach their full potential. He feels numb, every blow seems more painful and therefore he hangs back from tackles, which only increases his risk of injury. Extra clothes can help keep a player warm and a track suit or just a jersey and pair of trousers are very useful before the whistle blows for the kick-off. Vaseline or oil on exposed skin can also help but, as a means of helping players stay warm until movement in the heat of the match creates its own warmth, there is no substitute for vigorous exercise in the dressing room. Finally, remember not to let teams spend too much time outside before the kick-off. Keep an eye on the referee's changing room and on that of your opponents. Some managers have been known to let their opponents freeze for five or ten minutes before they let their team run out.

This advice is particularly important for the managers of boys' teams. Youngsters' ability to retain heat is not as effective as that of adults — they are much more at risk of hypothermia on the hills for example — and they can easily be chilled before the match starts.

## Loosening up
### Quadriceps muscles
The quadriceps muscle — the 'quads' — is a four-headed muscle, hence the name. Strip off so that you are naked from the waist down and look in a mirror. The quadriceps run from the line of the groin crease, down to the knee on the front of the thigh. Some fibres arise from the crest of the pelvis, others from the crutch and many rise from the thigh bone itself. All converge on the knee and many insert into the patella or knee cap (see page 82).

To loosen up the quadriceps bend one leg until the foot is near the buttock; reach down and catch the foot, now pull the foot up and back *slowly* and *gently* until you can feel the tension in the muscle. Now pull a little further, *slowly*, and relax. Repeat ten times.

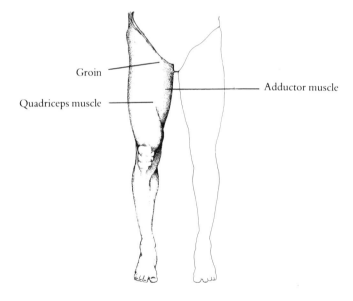

Fig. 5 Surface anatomy of the right leg showing the groin area, where the thigh meets the abdominal wall, and the well-developed part of the quadriceps groups of muscles running into the upper inner edge of the knee-cap which plays such an important part in stabilizing the knee joint.

*Hamstrings*

The hamstrings are a group of muscles which arise on the pelvis, from the points of bones on which you sit — reach down and feel. The muscles emerge from under the buttocks — stand up and feel how the buttock muscles sit on top of the hamstrings and run down the back of the thigh to the bones of the leg below the knee. Sit down again and feel behind your bent knee, tense and release your hamstrings and feel the tendons on the inner and outer margins of the hollow behind the knee by which the muscles transfer their power to the leg bones (see page 81). The hamstrings straighten the hip and bend the knee. It is very common for the hamstring muscle fibres to be torn loose from their attachments mainly because football players spend so much time concentrating on the strength of their quadriceps — the muscles on the front of the thigh. In kicking a ball these muscles exert a tremendous force on the bones of the leg to straighten the knee. This straightening of the knee requires the hamstrings to relax and lengthen as the thigh muscles contract and shorten. If the hamstrings are not in good condition they may not relax quickly enough and the fibres may tear away from their attachments.

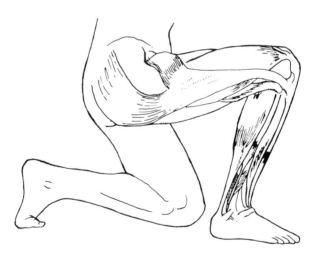

Fig. 6a  Diagrammatic view of muscles of right lower limb. Notice the hamstring muscle sweeping down to attach to the leg bone below the knee. These are the outer tendons which can be felt with the knee bent. Notice also the calf converging into tendons which run into the foot.

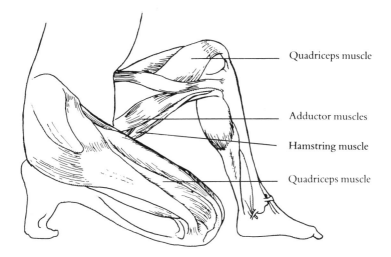

Fig. 6b Diagrammatic view of muscle of lower limbs. Notice the adductor muscle and the hamstring muscles inserting into the bones of the leg. These are the inner tendons which can be felt when the knee is bent.

Two exercises can slacken off the hamstrings and reduce the risk of a pulled hamstring. Stand up and bend forward slowly keeping the knees straight until you can feel your hamstrings under tension, now bend a little more, *gently* and *slowly*. Don't flap your body up and down like a puppet being jerked on strings; that looks impressive but is no use to your hamstrings and may in fact harm them.

The other method is to put one foot up on a table or bench about waist height with the knee straight. Lean forward until you can feel your hamstrings then stretch a little further like a hurdler but do it in *slow* and *gentle* motion. Again, don't pump your body back and forward, just reach forward *slowly* and *gently*. Repeat this ten times.

*Calf muscles*
These run from the back of the bones of the leg to the heel and they straighten the ankle joint; stand up, then rise on your toes and feel them working. They provide the drive when a player accelerates or jumps. Tears in the calf muscles can be prevented by muscular fitness and by slow stretching of the muscles before playing or training. Standing, place one foot well in front of the other, keeping both pointing directly forward, keep the back leg straight and bend the front knee, with the rear foot flat on the ground; you will soon feel the calf muscles under tension. Now pause, and then bend the

Fig. 7 Loosening up the hamstrings. The important feature of this exercise is *not* the bending of the player's trunk but the *slow and gentle* stretching of the hamstring muscles.
Fig. 8 Loosening up the hamstrings. The important feature of this exercise is *not* the forward bending of the player's trunk but a *slow and gentle* downward movement of the body which stretches the hamstring.

Fig. 9 Loosening up the calf muscles. The important feature of this exercise is that the player should stand with both feet pointing straight forward. If either foot is allowed to splay outward much of the benefit is lost.

front leg a little further *gently* and *slowly*, maintaining the body in an upright position. Repeat ten times.

*Adductors (groin muscles)*

Groin strains are a common problem, not surprisingly because the tissue where the quadriceps muscles blend into those of the abdominal wall is put under tremendous stress when kicking a football. Sometimes the pain which occurs in the groin area (the region of the obvious line where the abdominal muscles and quadriceps muscles meet) is actually above that line and is therefore a strain of the lower abdominal muscle. On other occasions it is a pull of the quadriceps muscle or one of the other thigh muscles. This can best be prevented by strengthening the lower abdominal muscles on each side. Most abdominal exercises, for example trunk curls, only strengthen the muscles in the midline but one type of exercise strengthens the lower abdomen. Lie on your back, raise one leg and one foot off the ground, swing it nine inches across the midline and hold it there. Now raise your trunk off the ground. This is a training exercise not a loosening up exercise, although it can be repeated very *slowly* and *gently* during loosening up.

The true groin strain hurts in the crutch where the muscles of the inner thigh meet the pelvic bones behind the scrotum. To loosen off these muscles stand with legs wide apart, feet facing straight forward. Then let one knee bend and let the body move gently to that side. This puts a tension on the adductor muscles on the other thigh. Feel the tension then *gently* and *slowly* stretch a little further. These are the most important muscles but don't forget three other groups of muscles:

1. Muscles on the outer aspects of the thigh. Stand with your feet apart, both feet pointing straight forward. Let your hand run down the outer aspect of one thigh slowly till you feel the bending of your body start to stretch the muscles on the outer aspect of the other thigh. Now bend a little further very *gently* and *slowly*.
2. Arms and shoulders. Circle one arm very *slowly*, stretching the shoulder muscles as much as possible.
3. Neck muscles. Put your hands on your hips, rotate the head very *slowly*, stretching it in every direction.

The muscles of boys are so supple that they do not need loosening up exercises, but from the age of fourteen or fifteen the performance of each exercise ten times should be strongly encouraged because older teenagers are often as inactive as adult players.

## Steaming up

Physical activity before a match can also help the players' psychological preparation. It is good to get players thinking about the task before them but it is also good to clear their minds of the game for a few minutes. This applies particularly to more nervous players. Physical activity can achieve this, especially physical activity which includes an element of competition. Pairing off with each couple taking it in turns to spar, one trying to hit the palms of the other held in front of him, or team competitions with three teams of four passing a ball back between their legs and returning it to the front by passing it above head height, usually raise the players' spirits. After leaving the dressing room some exercise which involves the whole team in a small tightly knit group is very useful not only to raise the team spirit and help nervous players, but also to impress the opposition.

Finally, remember the obvious saying that everyone is different. No two players are alike; some like to sit still and not speak, others are always chattering and on the make; each has his own style of mental preparation. Some use embrocation, others put their right boot on first. Some like Dextrosol, others, like a player who was a brilliant Scottish inside forward, a big glass of whisky, although we would not recommend this as a routine. The manager's job is to know his players, to let them be individuals but to ensure that each fulfils his potential.

### STIFFNESS

This is so common after exercise that it is often regarded as normal, but we prefer to regard it as an abnormal reaction, as a condition which can be prevented.

Stiffness is an accumulation of fluid in the muscles, between the muscle fibres. This fluid is contained within the fibrous cover of the muscle (see page 48), and because the fibrous tissue sheath is not elastic this build up increases the pressure inside the muscle, compressing the fibres which therefore contract more slowly. We described how the blood supply to the muscles increases during exercise (see page 33). The pressure inside these blood vessels rises to levels which are much higher than normal — feel how much more strongly your pulse beats in the neck after exercise — and some of the fluid in which the blood cells float leaks out into the muscles. In fit people most of the fluid which leaked out is reabsorbed and the best way to avoid stiffness is to become fit. In unfit people the blood vessels are not so effective and stiffness is much more common but its severity can always be reduced if two rules are observed: first *don't wallow in a hot bath*. A hot bath may feel very nice after a hard game, especially on a cold rainy day but it expands the blood vessels and causes more fluid to leak out. A quick shower or bath is better, followed by a cold shower or dip to contract the vessels. Secondly, *don't sit around unnecessarily*. After a training session it is important to 'wind down', to finish with a gentle period of exercise. The idea behind this is that gentle exercise helps restore fluid to the blood vessels. After an arduous game players will be too exhausted both physically and psychologically to wind down in this way — both mind and body are played out. Stiffness can be minimised however if players are encouraged to keep on the move. The most difficult situation for a manager is a long coach or train journey home after a game and players should be encouraged to walk the corridors or change seats regularly, especially if they have another match within forty-eight hours. If a player is stiff the morning after a game a waik or game of golf is an ideal antidote.

## CRAMP

When some muscle fibres fail to relax, that is when they go into cramp; the blood supply to them is cut off. This causes pain and in turn causes a nervous reflex to operate which contracts all the other fibres in the muscle, which causes more pain, which causes more cramp, in a vicious circle. No one knows exactly what is going on inside the muscle when it is in cramp, or why it goes into cramp and, therefore, no one has worked out a cure for cramp. However, the vicious cycle can be broken by *stretching* the muscle which is cramped. This blocks the nervous reflex, reduces the cramp, which allows more blood to flow, which reduces the pain and allows the muscle fibres to mobilise their energy stores. Once more the secret of treatment is *slowly* to stretch the cramped muscle and hold it stretched.

### Calf cramp
To find out how to stretch a player's calf muscle find out how to stretch your own. Sit down on the floor, legs out in front of you, flat on the ground, feet together. Now bend your feet back towards you; you will immediately feel the stretch on your calf muscles. To

stretch another person's muscles — find someone to practice on now — make the person sit with legs flat, kneel on the same side as the leg which has cramp. Take the heel of the affected leg in your hand — right hand for right leg, left hand for left leg. Allow the sole of the foot to rest along your forearm, now move your forearm so that the foot is bent *gently* back, keeping the heel on the ground and the knee flat. *Don't* put your other hand on the knee cap. In practice, first untie the player's tie-up then use this technique. Cramp should quickly relax. If the muscle goes into cramp as soon as you release your hold, stretch it again *slowly* and *gently*. When the muscle has relaxed you may massage the whole muscle; support the muscle in your hand like you would hold a baby's head, don't dig into it with your finger tips. The application of an ice-pack or cold sponge (see page 111) to a muscle in cramp is also effective and can be tried either before or after the slow stretch.

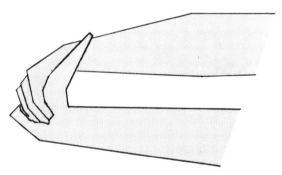

Fig. 10  Relief of calf cramp by holding the player's heel in the cupped hand — right hand for right leg — and bending the foot back slowly, gently and firmly. Be careful not to press on the toes or the forefoot as this reduces the effectiveness of the technique.

### Hamstring cramp

We have already described how to stretch your hamstring when loosening up. To relieve hamstring cramp a different technique is needed. Lie on the floor, bend one hip as far as you can so that your thigh touches your abdomen; your knee will be bent as a result of this. Now straighten your knee and feel your hamstrings stretch. This is what you must try to do when a player has cramp. To stretch someone else's hamstring, kneel beside him on the same side as the affected side. Hold the foot by allowing it to rest between your thumb and index finger — right hand, right foot, as before. Now, keeping the knee bent, bend the hip so that you are holding the person's lower limb with the hip and knee bent. Then straighten the knee slowly and gently. Again an ice-bag is very useful in the treatment of hamstring cramp.

Fig. 11 Hamstring muscles being slowly stretched.

## Foot cramp
Cramp in the arch of the foot is very painful. To treat it, press up on the ball of the foot or put the foot in a bucket of cold water.

### CONTUSION — DEAD LEG

Boys seldom suffer from the muscle pulls and stresses which affect older players but there is one type of muscle injury which affects players of all ages — a dead leg. This is the result of a blow on a muscle from a boot or knee. The result is severe pain localised to the area at which the blow struck, and the player falls to the ground. What has happened inside the muscle is that a number of blood vessels have been broken and the blood leaks out from the torn ends just as in a black eye. The tissue round the eye is slack and a large amount of blood can leak out with relatively little pain. In muscle tissue, however, the fibres are very tightly packed together and any blood which leaks out forces fibres aside and a pool of blood forms which puts all the surrounding tissues under pressure. This causes pain and thus causes the muscle to go into spasm. The problem then is one of bleeding and the principles of treatment are the same as if the bleeding was coming from a skin cut — elevation, cold and pressure (see page 10).

1. *Elevation* — take the player off, and raise the painful part above the level of the heart. If the blow has been severe don't let the player back to the field of play. Take him to the dressing room, on a stretcher if possible, and keep the leg elevated until he can be taken home. When at home the player should, but often won't, lie with his leg elevated for at least twenty-four hours, until Sunday afternoon after a Saturday match. The worst thing to do is to stand all night drinking or dancing after such an injury.

2. *Cold* — again there is a need to be careful about the use of ice (see page111)but an ice-pack or ice cubes or, better, crushed ice in a polythene bag will make blood vessels constrict; a sponge with cold water is almost as good. The player must not have a hot bath. This can make the bleeding worse.

3. *Pressure* — great care must be taken not to apply too much pressure on top of the damaged area as this can merely make the blood spread farther away from the site of bleeding. In clubs with the service of a qualified doctor or physiotherapist this type of injury is commonly bound in a pressure bandage — layers of crepe and cotton wool — but we would not advise anyone who has not been properly trained to attempt to apply a pressure bandage. Rely on elevation and cold.

This type of injury usually heals quickly but a painful lump may persist for weeks or even months. Avoid the temptation of trying to knead the lump like a lump of dough. This can aggravate the problem. Very gentle rubbing, like stroking the cat, is all that should be tried. If pain persists for more than two weeks consult a physiotherapist or a doctor.

# 7.
# FOOT PROBLEMS

## The individual's contribution

Few parts of the body are so ignored as a player's feet. Many players spend a great deal of time bandaging ankles or rubbing embrocation into thigh muscles, activities which are rarely of much use, but few are prepared to take the few minutes necessary to look after their feet, minutes which can prevent not only the loss of hours and weeks of playing time but also pain and disability in later life long after playing days are over.

Athlete's foot and blisters can be prevented by careful washing and drying of the feet after every occasion on which they become sweaty. This means at least once a day. Feet should be washed in warm water and should be washed quickly. Nothing is worse than soaking them for ages in very hot water — just look at boiled ham! The feet should be dried gently but thoroughly and this is helped by leaving them exposed to the air for a few minutes after finishing with the towel before putting shoes on. Talcum powder is very useful but is no substitute for careful drying, especially between the toes. Socks should be changed daily and football socks should be washed each time they are used. Nylon socks should be discouraged for both playing and everyday wear as they increase sweating.

If the skin becomes hard it may crack and a little lanolin, which is available from the pharmacist, should be rubbed in if patches of skin are becoming hard. Not too much should be used, just enough to cover the palm of the hand, and it should be rubbed in no more than twice a week. Nail care is of great importance. Nails should be cut straight across but sharp projecting corners which dig into neighbouring toes should be taken off with a file. If a player has problems with his toe nails, for example redness or pain at the side or base of the nails, or difficulty with cutting them satisfactorily, a chiropodist should be consulted (see page 19).

In addition, to help skin, nails, bones and joints, players should be encouraged to wear shoes which do not cramp the toes or foot. Boots, fortunately, are usually chosen with more care than shoes and do not give rise to foot problems as often as faulty shoes do. The boot should fit closely but should not crowd the toes together. If a player complains of pain in the part of the foot near the toes or develops a painful corn on top of a toe, or has recurrent problems with his feet, suspect his boots. The soles should be flat inside the boot and not deformed. The studs should be well maintained so that the boot stands level when placed on a flat surface and they should be changed if the player starts to go over on the uppers.

Boot problems pose particular difficulties for the managers of boys' teams. The feet of a growing boy require footwear which allows room for development but many parents — particularly single mothers or unemployed fathers — may not be able to afford new boots or shoes as often as is necessary. The purchase of boots is a better use for club funds than tracksuits or continental tours, yet footwear, like feet, are often ignored when teams are being kitted out.

## The coach's contribution

Coaches and managers can contribute to good foot care by keeping a big tin of talcum in the travelling bag, encouraging players to take good care of their feet and, perhaps most important of all, ensuring that players wash their socks and wear clean socks for every match or training session. Too many managers concentrate on kit from the knee up and ignore the player's socks. Those who organise boys' teams face particular difficulties. Some parents are insulted by the suggestion that their son does not have his socks washed often enough. Others will maintain that they cannot afford to buy new shoes often enough to give growing feet room and that those shoes which they buy have to be made of artificial material rather than leather, again because of price. This will be true in some cases. In others, it will be obvious to the coach that the parents have got sufficient money but prefer to spend it on things other than boys' shoes and this can be a difficult subject for the coach to discuss with such parents.

No matter how hard the coach works to prevent foot problems, however, some will occur and they must be carefully treated.

### BLISTERS

A blister is a collection of fluid under the surface of the skin. The fluid may be blood-stained but a blood blister is not more serious than one which contains clear fluid. The release of fluid in a blister should be carried out using a sterilised needle as soon as it is the size of a penny in diameter. Soak a needle in hydrogen peroxide for two minutes or hold it in the hottest part of the flame of a match until it is red hot to sterilise it. Then insert the needle through the skin overlying the fluid, pushing it, in parallel to the surface of the blister, for about 3 millimetres. Then lift the needle upwards to make a good opening. This will not cause pain. If the blister bursts spontaneously and there is a loose flap of skin catch hold of the flap with tweezers and cut if off with scissors. In the healing stage of a blister it helps to expose the raw surface to the air as much as possible and to elevate the foot, because that reduces the tendency for fluid to seep out of the blood vessels underlying the raw area. If the player takes of his shoe and sock when watching television and puts the foot up on a chair it will help the skin cells to re-cover the raw surface. There is no point in trying to harden the skin of the foot by artificial means in an attempt to prevent blisters. Paddling in the sea is beneficial for those lucky enough to live near the seaside but players should be discouraged from trying to pickle their feet. The best means of preventing blisters is to follow the advice on prevention given in the previous section, paying particular attention to the feet in hot weather, for example during early season training.

## ATHLETE'S FOOT

Athlete's foot is caused by a fungus which flourishes on sweaty skin. It can be prevented by following the rules of good foot care but even the most careful person can become infected. The infection spreads readily from person to person and this causes a problem for the coach or trainer when one player is infected. Cross infection from one player to another can be prevented if the player with an infection is asked to use the shower last and does not share a communal bath with other players. The infected player should also stand on a towel, which should be used for no other purpose, and should not walk in his bare feet on surfaces used by other players. Also, when there is a source of infection in the squad all the other members should take even more care of their feet than usual.

Athlete's foot is a condition with red and scaly areas of skin between the toes, and may occur on the soles of the feet only with painful cracks under the toes. It is an extremely itchy condition and the itchiness may be the first sign of infection. Two preparations can be bought from the chemist for the treatment of Athlete's foot: *Tinaderm* and *Tineafax*. Both are equally effective and available in powder and cream forms. Both powder and cream should be bought. The cream should be applied between all the toes twice a day and the powder should be used to dust the socks. Cotton socks must be worn during the treatment period.

If there is no improvement after two weeks of treatment a doctor should be consulted.

## VERRUCAS AND CORNS

A verruca is a type of wart which occurs on the sole of the foot. It is usually noticed as a painful lump and may be mistakenly diagnosed as a corn by the sufferer. A corn is a thickening of natural skin, quite different from a wart, which is an abnormal growth in the skin caused by a viral infection. A verruca can usually be fairly easily distinguished from a corn because it always occurs on the sole of the foot and has a clear line round the area of hard skin, whereas a corn merges into the normal skin round it and often occurs on top of a toe. If there is any doubt a chiropodist should be consulted. A corn can be treated by using lanolin and by abrading it with an emery board — a cardboard nail file — but a verucca requires specialist treatment. Because a verruca is caused by a virus it can be spread from one person to another and any player who suffers from a verruca should not walk barefoot on the same surfaces as other players. He should bathe separately or wear plastic sandals if he uses the same showers.

## PAINFUL FEET

### Acute pain

If a player has his foot stood on or kicked and develops pain which can be localised to one spot, either on a toe or over one of the bones of the arch of the foot, a fracture should be suspected. It is, as always when a fracture is suspected, helpful to ask the player to point with one finger to the point at which the pain is greatest. Locate the comparable point on the other foot if you are in doubt whether or not there is a bone underlying the point indicated by the player. Occasionally a player develops a localised acute pain in the arch of the foot while running without having had his foot kicked or stood on. This type of pain can be caused by a spontaneous fracture of one of the bones of the foot. The bone fractures due to fatigue just as a metal axle can fracture.

If you think that someone has fractured a bone in his foot take off his boot, elevate his foot to as high a level as possible above the head by lying the player on his back and wrap the foot gently in a cold wet towel or put the whole foot in a bucket of very cold water for at least ten minutes. This reduces the bleeding inside the foot, reduces the tension of the tissues and therefore reduces the pain. If a broken bone is suspected the player should be transported to the accident department of the nearest hospital keeping his foot as high as possible.

## Chronic pain

To understand chronic foot pain, that is pain which occurs continually or intermittently over a period of weeks or months without a fracture being present, it is necessary to appreciate the anatomy of the foot. Put your feet in a basin of water and stand on a surface which shows up the foot marks clearly.

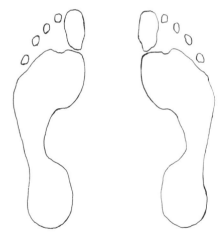

Fig. 12 Footprints showing that each foot is an arch from heel to toe and that the two feet together form an arch from the outer border of one foot to the outer border of the other.

Each foot has an arch from toe to heel, commonly called the arch of the foot. But the two feet together also form a complete arch from side to side with each foot forming half an arch from the inside, where the half arch is at its highest, to the outer border of the foot which rests on the ground. The shape of the bones which comprise the foot help to maintain these arches just as the shape of the stones cut in a cathedral arch help preserve the arch.

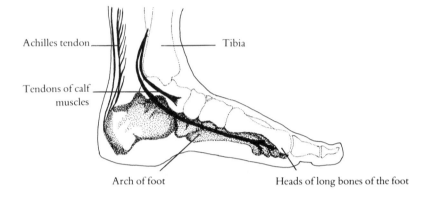

Fig. 13 Drawing of the bones of the foot viewed from the inner aspect. Note the Achilles tendon joining on the heel bone and the two tendons which run under the lower end of the tibia. One of the tendons runs right across the arch of the foot and helps preserve the shape of the arch by tying the two ends together.

However the arches are not maintained by the shape of the bones alone. Three other types of structure maintain their shape:

1. Ligaments joining each of the bones of the foot to all its neighbouring bones.
2. Tendons running from the calf muscles across the sole of the foot which tie the lower points of the arches together, like beams tie retaining walls together.
3. Muscles which arise in the sole of the foot from bones just in front of the heel and run forward to insert into the bones of the forefoot and toes.

When one or more of the small ligaments or muscles tear the arches start to sag and this causes pain. There may be no sensation of tearing, that is no acute pain, because the ligaments and muscles may stretch slowly over the course of years so that the player is gradually affected by an aching in his feet as he gets older particularly after training in a gym or on hard ground. The pain may be localised high up in the arch of the foot or in the forefoot where the long bones of the foot meet the toes. (This area is analogous to the knuckles of the hand). As the ligaments and muscles which hold the forefoot together stretch, the bones spread apart and the 'heads' of the long bones, the end where they meet the bones of the toes, come much closer to the skin and therefore the ground. The heads of the bones are no longer protected by a pad of tissue and this causes pain.

If, in addition, the toes have been crowded together in cramped shoes or boots the joints are further distorted. The joint most frequently affected is that at the base of the big toe. It may become angled — a condition called *Hallux Valgus* — and a bunion may form on top of the bony prominence formed by the unnatural angle. A bunion is a protective cushion of tissue laid down by the body to reduce the frictional pressure on the bony joint but even though its primary function is protective, it can become inflamed and painful.

Anyone with chronic foot pain which lasts more than two weeks should consult a chiropodist. Paddling in the sea and walking in bare feet can help, but it really requires the skill of a chiropodist to prescribe treatment specifically suited to the precise cause of the problem. Treatment usually consists of making pads to support those parts of the arch which are most affected and advice on exercises to strengthen the muscles of the feet and the muscles of the calf which, through their tendons, help to maintain the arches of the foot.

The other part of the foot in which chronic pain occurs is around the heel. Pain may arise in three sites:

1. Under the heel: the bone which forms the heel is separated from the skin by only a thin layer of tissue — feel it on your own foot. Bruising can develop on the under surface of the heel bone. This occurs most commonly after playing on hard grounds. The player should try to avoid playing or training until the pain has gone and may find a heel pad made from Dr. Scholl's material, which is available in most pharmacists, helpful. If it persists a chiropodist should be consulted.

2. At the back of the heel bone: this pain is due to friction between the skin overlying the heel bone and a boot or shoe. This is another area in which the bone comes very near the surface and is poorly padded — feel it on your own foot. Blisters may develop or a thickening of soft tissue which may also be called a bunion. Try padding the offending boot or shoe or changing to another design which puts less pressure on the particular point of pain and consult a chiropodist if these measures fail.

3. At the back of the ankle just above the heel bone: this type of pain is due to minor tears of the Achilles tendon where it joins the bone or inflammation around the tendon. Rest is the best treatment but a small pad *under* the heel can be tried. If the pain does not go after two weeks without playing or training a physiotherapist or chiropodist should be consulted (see Achilles tendon injuries page 50).

# 8.
# ANKLE AND LEG INJURIES

## THE MORTICE AND TENON JOINT

Take off your socks and shoes. Run you right thumb down the shin
bone — the tibia — until it comes to rest on the knob of bone at the
lower end. Now remove your thumb, and feel for the other bone
which runs between knee and ankle — the fibula — which lies on
the outer aspect of the leg. It is covered by more muscle than the
shin bone but can be located easily if you start from the knob of
bone on the *outside* of the ankle and work upwards feeling the fibula
which ends in a knob of bone about two inches below the knee. Put
your thumb on the lower end of the tibia and your little finger on
the lower end of the fibula and your hand illustrates the bony
arrangement which forms the tenon for the mortice of the foot to fit
into, for the ankle is a mortice and tenon joint. The tibia and fibula

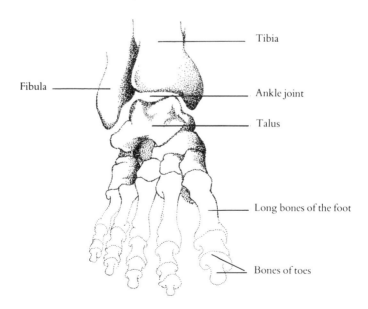

Fig. 14 The bones of the right ankle joint. Notice how the end of the fibula extends lower
than the end of the tibia.

are bound together by ligaments, as the bones of the palm of the hand are bound together, and these ligaments prevent the two bones spreading apart, thus providing a secure bony and ligamentous socket into which the bones of the foot fit. The joint between the foot and the tibia and fibula is surrounded by a fibrous capsule and this is thickened on the inside and the outside, or in medical terms on the medial and lateral sides, to form ligaments. Allow your thumb to slide down just below the lower end of the tibia and feel the space between that bone and the prominent bone on the medial side of the foot. Move the foot to make the distinction between tibia and foot clearer. These two points of bones are bound together by the medial ligament of the ankle which is a thick band of fibrous tissue.

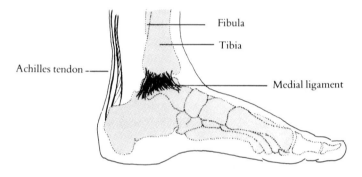

Fig. 15 Diagrammatic view of the inner aspect of the ankle showing the fan-shaped medial ligament running from the lower end of the tibia to the bones of the foot.

Now move your little finger to the space below the lower end of the fibula and feel the space between it and the bones of the foot. The space between the fibula and the bones of the foot is crossed by the lateral ligaments which run from the lower and internal face of this prominence of bone to the foot. These are the lateral ligaments of the ankle and they are narrow fibrous cords, which can usually be felt if the foot is tilted inwards.

The stability of the ankle joint is further strengthened by the tendons which run from the leg to the foot. At the back of the ankle the Achilles tendon supports the joint and, in front of it, tendons run from the leg behind and beneath the ankle to the sole of the foot and the toes. On the outer, or lateral, side of the ankle tendons run under the prominent spur of bone at the lower end of the fibula. They run from the muscles covering the fibula to the bones of the foot — move the foot up and down and feel them as you do so. The tendons of the muscles on the front of the leg run to the toes across the front of the ankle joint. With your thumb and little finger on the lower ends of tibia and fibula respectively raise your toes up and back towards you and feel the taut tendons spring into prominence under your hand. These tendons are bound down by strong fibres running across the front of the ankle just under the skin. The tendons are like hawsers and the horizontal fibres which bind them down are like a pulley round which the tendons change direction. From this band of strong transverse fibres other fibres run downwards and outwards across the top of the foot to the outer border of the foot. The direction of these fibres is demonstrated by the direction your three other fingers take as they lie across the top of the foot.

It is essential to understand these points to appreciate the most common type of ankle injury — the inversion injury.

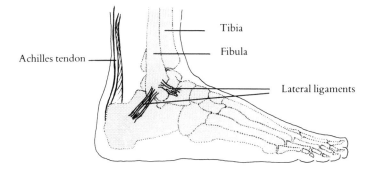

Fig. 16 Diagrammatic view of the outer aspect of the ankle showing two of the lateral ligaments which run from the lower end of the fibula to the bones of the foot.

INVERSION INJURIES

**Assessment and early management**

Very few people manage to play football for any length of time without suffering an inversion injury to the ankle joint. By inversion is meant a movement of the foot downwards *and* inwards. Try it now and feel where the strain is greatest. It is, of course, on the fibres which fan out across the top of the foot and, if you really push the foot down and inwards, on the lateral ligaments. The player usually reports that he has 'gone over' his ankle when he sustains this type of injury. The pain is caused by the fibres tearing loose from their attachments. This is followed by swelling, which results from the leakage of blood from the blood vessels which are torn by the sudden stretching, and the swelling itself causes further pain as it stretches and disrupts the normal arrangement of tissues.

If the tear is a minor one the player will usually be able to rise and play on but we believe that any player who sustains an inversion injury should be substituted unless there are *very* important reasons why he should stay on. The use of a spray or, just as effective, a sponge soaked in cold water, held over the sock can reduce the pain quite quickly but if the player returns to the game the bleeding will continue at a much greater rate than if he comes off. This causes more swelling, pain and discomfort, which develops after the match is over and the boot has been taken off, and more disruption of the tissues of the foot which therefore take longer to heal. In general we believe that the player should be taken off and then the three steps necessary to stop bleeding can be taken quickly and effectively:

1. Elevation — raise the ankle above the level of the heart so that gravity empties the blood vessels (see page 10). Lie the player down on his back and put his foot up on a bench or on a low table. Place it on a pad and support the foot on either side so that it does not move from side to side.
2. Cold — apply a cold sponge or ice-bag (see page 111) or put the whole foot in a bucket of cold water for ten minutes before elevation.
3. Pressure — the pressure necessary to maintain the sponge or ice-bag in position will be sufficient. There is no need to bind the ankle.

If the inversion injury involves only a few fibres this treatment will be sufficient but the player must continue with elevation for at least twenty-four hours. There is little point in taking these steps in the early stage of the injury if the player intends to stand about in a pub or go to a disco later on because the bleeding will occur then.

If the injury is more serious, medical advice is necessary. The severity of an inversion injury is best assessed by comparing the ankle with the other, undamaged, ankle and following the simple rules — Look and Listen before you Touch.

1. Look for any obvious deformity in the bony structure and observe the amount of swelling. If the injury is severe the bleeding can be considerable in a minute or two. In minor injuries it usually takes some time to develop. If there is considerable swelling very soon after the injury you should

   seek the advice of a doctor that same day (see page 22).

2. Listen to what the player says about how the injury happened and where it hurts most. Ask him to indicate with one finger exactly where the pain is most severe, and to point out the same spot on the other ankle. Ask him if he can stand on the ankle. After ten minutes have passed a player should be able to put weight on the ankle. If he cannot, a fracture should be suspected and the player should be taken to hospital.

3. Touch the other ankle first and try to decide in your own mind exactly where the pain is worst. If it is *on* the lower end of the fibula, on the bone, there may be a fracture and the player should see a doctor *as soon as possible*. If it is immediately *in front of or below* the fibula a ligament may be torn and a doctor should be seen *as soon as possible*. If it is further forward or lower it is probable that the injury is minor and a doctor need not be consulted unless the swelling is very great or the player is in severe pain.

## Returning to action

If the player has sustained a fracture or has torn a ligament and has been attending a hospital he will receive advice from the physiotherapist or doctor about returning to training and playing. If the inversion injury was minor, however, and has been treated by you and the player himself, the decision as to when he can start training again has to be made by the player with your help and it is not an easy decision. After the player has been free from pain for a week while walking about normally he may be allowed to start training, but should do nothing except very gentle jogging and should *not* play a game or kick a ball. After a week of this level of activity he can increase the strain, provided that he has not had any twinges of pain, and gradually build up his activity until he is able to return to play.

   The part which strapping can play in supporting the ankle during the recovery phase and in preventing a recurrence of the injury is difficult to assess. It certainly helps the player psychologically if his ankle is bound or if he wears an anklet and probably helps during gentle exercise, but the only support which could hold an ankle subjected to the degree of stress imposed during a game is a solid cast made of plaster of paris and no-one would play well with this type of support! In spite of our reservations it is worthwhile knowing how to apply strapping to the ankle because it has some physical benefit. But you must be careful to remember that strapping is not a substitute for normal healing and to ensure that a player does not use strapping to return to play before he is able to run and kick a ball without strapping and without pain. We realise that this advice is a counsel of perfection. Players will often 'take a chance' and managers may also be forced to play someone who has not reached the level of recovery we have laid down as being desirable. We deplore the practice which has developed in some countries of injecting pain killing drugs into an ankle, or other joints, to allow a player to take the field, but realise that sometimes people will play when they have not fully recovered. We ourselves have broken the rule we have laid down but believe it is right to set this high standard if only to make a person who breaks the rule, either player or manager, realise that what he is doing may have harmful consequences. Never forget that pain is a useful sensation. It may seem pointless but its function is to warn the person that something is wrong.

There are many ways of strapping the ankle. There is no one method which is 'the right way'. All have their advantages and disadvantages but here is the one which we use:

1. Shave the leg.
2. Apply a strip of one-inch sticking plaster to the leg. Loop it under the arch of the foot and pull it up each side of the leg.
3. Repeat this, overlapping the first length of strapping by half an inch.
4. Apply more strips until the strips nearly meet in the mid line.
5. Apply shorter lengths of strapping to the foot.
6. Bind the strapping to the leg by some horizontal strips but do not wrap tape round and round the calf muscles.

We believe this to be better than strapping by completely surrounding the foot and leg, as this can interfere with the blood supply to the foot and toes, but if you find the method we have described unsatisfactory use three-inch tape and bind the foot and ankle. Commence the strapping by laying the tape on the inner aspect of the ankle then run it under the arch of the foot and pull it up over the lateral, or outer, side of the ankle. Then wind it round the ankle and repeat the figure of eight pattern several times.

To become proficient it is necessary to practice and practice on yourself and on other coaches, your wife, girlfriend, or anyone else who will put up with it. Once you have applied strapping to yourself try it out by wearing it for ninety minutes during a game or training session. You will probably find that the strapping is un-

satisfactory and annoying after forty-five minutes, unless you have
had the opportunity to practice a great deal under expert supervision. We believe that many coaches will find it easier to encourage
their players to discuss their problems with a physiotherapist (see
page 18) or pharmacist (see page 22) and buy an anklet of supportive
elastic.

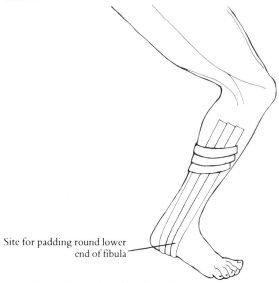

Site for padding round lower
end of fibula

Fig. 17 Strapping of the ankle joint with one inch tape — in practice more vertical strips
would be applied than are shown. (It may be necessary to apply a pad under the prominence
of bone at the lower end of the fibula). Notice how the transverse strips run upwards and
forwards and they they do not completely encircle the leg.

## POTT'S FRACTURE

Turn your foot upwards and outwards, in a direction opposite to
inversion; you will find that there is a much smaller range of
movement than there is in inversion — invert your foot to check
this. The reason is that the lower end of the fibula extends about half
an inch lower than the lower end of the tibia so that when the foot
starts to move upwards and outwards its progress is very soon
halted by a lump of bone, which is not the case when it moves
downwards and inwards. If the movement of the foot as it turns
upwards and outwards is of great force both the tibia and the fibula
may be damaged.

   The lower end of the fibula may be smashed off as the bone of the
foot crashes against it. As the foot moves rapidly away from the

tibia it may tear off the medial ligament, and sometimes a chip of bone, as it does so. This is called a Pott's fracture after Sir Percival Pott, who first described it.

A Pott's fracture is not uncommon in football, for example when a player kicks a ball which is blocked by another player's leg, and should be suspected when a player complains of pain on both the inside and the outside of his ankle.

Again the rule is Look and Listen before you Touch:

1. Look for the sites at which swelling is occurring — swelling which develops a few minutes after injury should make you suspect a fracture. Compare the damaged ankle to the normal one.

2. Listen to the player's description of his injury and ask him to indicate with one finger exactly where the pain is greatest.

3. Touch the other ankle to try to determine where the pain is greatest.

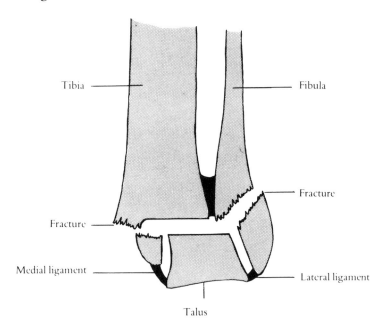

Fig. 18 Pott's fracture. The left ankle viewed from in front. The foot has been forced outwards against the lower end of the fibula causing fracture in it and pulling the tip off the lower end of the tibia.

## CHIPPED ANKLE BONES

Direct violence to the ankle in the form of a kick can cause a fracture at the point of contact. Listen to the player's account of the injury. Look at the point he indicates as being the most painful and touch either it or the comparable point on the undamaged ankle. If it is on a bone and the pain persists more than ten minutes in spite of the application of cold — just squeeze a sponge of cold water over it if it is too painful to allow an ice-pack to be held to it.

If a fracture is suspected take the player to see a doctor *as soon as possible* and *do not give him anything to eat or drink.*


## BROKEN LEGS

The diagnosis of a broken leg is usually easy to make because the crack can be heard all round the ground and the player falls immediately and is unable to rise. A careful look reveals that his leg is deformed. (Very painful swelling can occur over the shin bone where it lies immediately under the skin without a fracture being present. If the player can stand up within ten minutes of such an injury a fracture is very unlikely.)

If you suspect a fracture don't meddle, put the player on a stretcher, supporting the leg on both sides of the suspected fracture as you lift him on. It is now possible to buy an inflatable splint which provides excellent support. This is a double layer of plastic shaped like a Wellington boot with a zip running up the front. Air can be introduced between the two layers of plastic by blowing into a valve. The foot and ankle are placed in the open splint which is zipped up and inflated (see page 108). If you buy this type of splint for your club, practice putting it on before you have to attempt putting it on someone with a fracture. Experiment with your wife or girlfriend and don't wait until you are faced with a fracture before you use it for the first time.

*Remember not to give someone who might have a fracture anything to eat or drink* because he may require a general anaesthetic soon after arrival at hospital.

## PREVENTION

The trainer or manager can reduce the risk of ankle and leg injuries by:

1. Ensuring that players wear well fitting boots.
2. Guarding the ankle against kicks with an extra pair of socks (see page 40) or by strapping cotton wool round the ankle.
3. Encouraging or, in the case of boys' teams, demanding that all players wear shin pads.
4. Encouraging the development of skills and muscle fitness. The former keep ankles out of trouble and fitness of the muscles which support the ankles reduces the risk of inversion injuries.

Players and managers can only do so much. They also have to rely on the referee and linesmen because tackling over the top is, regrettably, still a common cause of injured ankles and legs.

Once more we would encourage managers and coaches to think of prevention and to ask themselves every time they have to deal with an injured ankle not only 'how should I treat this injury?' but 'why did it happen and can I prevent it happening to other players?'.

# 9.
# KNEE INJURIES

## BASIC ANATOMY

Some joints are stable because the bones fit into one another. The hip joint is a stable ball and socket joint which is very rarely injured at football. The ankle joint is a mortice and tenon joint and obtains some stability from this arrangement. The bones of the knee-joint do not give this stability because it consists of a round surface, the lower end of the femur, resting on a flat surface, the upper surface of the tibia.

The knee joint, therefore, relies much less on the bones to preserve its stability than other joints do. It relies much more on the three other structures which act as stablizers in all joints: ligaments, muscles and tendons.

Take your trousers off, provided that you are not in a place where this might lead to your arrest, and try to feel the knee-joint. If you press your fingers in on either side of the knee-cap (the patella) and move your knee you should be able to feel where the thigh bone — the femur — meets the shin bone — the tibia. Stop moving your knee and try to feel the line of the joint, which feels like a groove, as it runs backwards on either side of the knee. You will not be able to feel it all round the joint because of the ligaments, tendons and muscles.

## Ligaments
The knee has four main ligaments. Two are right in the centre of the joint, and cannot be felt, but two are just under the skin. The medial ligament, which is on the inside of the knee about half way between front and back, consists of a thick sheet of fibres and cannot be easily identified with your fingers except by feeling where the groove of the joint becomes less easy to define. The lateral ligament is more cord-like and can be usually felt.

## Tendons
The hamstring muscles run from the bones of the pelvis, under the muscles of the buttocks, to the knee (see page 47). Before they reach the knee they become fibrous tendons, like wire hawsers running from an engine to the point at which the power generated by the engine is needed. Sitting with your knee bent reach behind your knee and feel the tendons running to attach to the tibia. You can feel

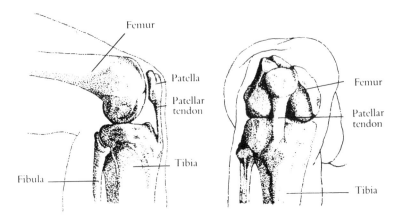

Fig. 19 Knee, bent — outside view showing the small area of femur which rests on the tibia when the knee is fully flexed.

Fig. 20 Knee, bent — front view showing the attachment of the patellar tendon to the tibia.

one tendon on the outer side of the knee and a group of tendons on the inner with a hollow between them. In front of the knee below the knee-cap is the patellar tendon. Sit down on the floor and stretch your leg out in front of you. Place one hand over the thigh muscle (quadriceps) on the same side. Now run your hand over the muscle and feel as it narrows just above the knee-cap — this is the quadriceps tendon. Let your thigh muscles relax and feel how this tendon, the knee-cap and the patellar tendon which joins the knee-cap to the tibia function as one unit. They are in fact all parts of one tendon structure; the knee-cap is merely a pulley allowing the tendon to ride round the bony end of the thigh bone without fraying and snapping. With the thigh muscle relaxed it is easy to move the patella from side to side. When the muscle is contracted the tendon is taut above and below the patella and it cannot be moved from side to side.

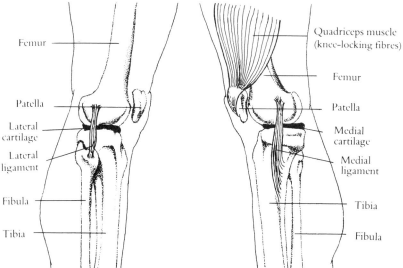

Fig. 21 Diagrammatic view of the important structures on the inner aspect of the knee joint. Note the powerful **band of** quadriceps muscle sweeping into the upper inner edge of the knee-cap. These are the fibres which tighten during the last few degrees of knee straightening. Note also the medial ligament of the knee joint and the medial cartilage depicted in black between the femur and the tibia.

Fig. 22 Diagrammatic view of the important structures on the outer aspect of the knee joint. Note that the fibula, the smaller of the two leg bones, does not make contact with the femur but is joined to it by the lateral ligament of the knee joint. The lateral cartilage is depicted in black between the two bones.

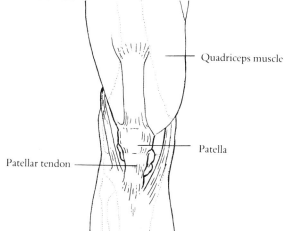

Fig. 23 Diagrammatic representation of patella showing the muscle fibres converging into the knee-cap from the quadriceps and the patellar tendons running from the knee-cap to the tibia. Notice how some fibres sweep down and round both sides of the patella to attach directly into the tissues of the leg.

## Muscles

The contribution of the tendons to the stability of the knee joint depends mostly on the strength of the muscles from which they originate. It is the tension in them, rather than just the physical presence of the tendons which is important. There are also some muscles which actually cross the joint line themselves and do not transmit their power by tendons; they make a direct contribution to the stability of the joint. Behind and just below the bent knee you can easily feel muscles between the tendons of the hamstrings. These are the calf muscles, running from the lower end of the back of the femur to the Achilles tendon. They are important but much less so than the quadriceps muscles, the most important part of which is the piece which runs towards and attaches to the upper, inner border of the knee-cap. This piece of muscle, which is very well developed in fit footballers, is of vital importance in stabilizing the knee and therefore in preventing knee injuries. Swing your knee under the chair on which you are sitting and then bring it up and forward until it is straight. Put your fingers on the front of the tibia and feel how the tibia rotates inwards during the last few degrees of straightening. The muscle fibres of this part of the quadriceps contract during these last few degrees of straightening to lock the bones in their most stable position. Repeat this movement slowly several times. Really concentrate on what is happening; feel the knee lock firmly as it straightens and, with your thumb, feel the locking muscle become firm only during the last few degrees. An understanding of this is essential if the principles of treating knee injuries are to be understood.


## ACUTE PAIN

Pain which comes on suddenly is usually the result of a kick or knock, or is due to damage to ligaments or to structures within the joint called cartilages.

## Kicks

Few blows are more painful than a direct blow on the knee-cap. The sickening crack echoes round the ground and the player falls as though he has been shot. Take the player off and pour cold water over the knee-cap by squeezing a sponge over it — it will usually be too painful to apply a cold sponge or ice-bag directly. If the pain does not reduce to a level which allows the player to return to play within ten minutes the player may have suffered a fracture of the knee-cap and he should be taken to hospital *as soon as possible*.

## Torn ligaments

It is not uncommon for players to complain of 'tweaks' or 'twinges' in the knee during the course of play. They feel 'something give', experience pain of short duration, then recover as they play on. Such episodes are probably due to minor tears in the fibrous tissue which surrounds the knee-joint. They can be ignored but if the pain persists after the game apply the basic treatment for bleeding: cold, elevation and gentle pressure.

If a player tears a ligament the picture is completely different. The damage is usually sustained when players clash, particularly if one player clatters into another in such a way that the knee is forced sideways. The player falls and has severe pain on either the inner or outer aspect of the knee, or has severe pain which affects the whole knee so that he is unable to localise it precisely. He is unable to rise or put weight on the leg and swelling becomes obvious within thirty minutes, as blood leaks into the joint from torn blood vessels. Always compare an injured knee with the undamaged knee and ask the player to indicate the point at which the pain is greatest if he can do so. Remember the golden rule — Look and Listen before you Touch. If the pain is severe, the player should not be sent back to play; he will rarely be able to anyway. The knee should be elevated, even six inches above ground level will be helpful provided that the player lies his body flat so that his knee is above the level of his heart. Try to support the whole leg while it is elevated and do not merely elevate the foot, because this puts a strain on the knee. Keep the knee wrapped in a cold damp towel or apply a compression bandage (see page 12). If the bleeding is so great that the knee is swollen and tense by the end of the match take the player to hospital *as soon as possible*. The doctor will usually X-ray the knee to exclude the possibility of a fracture, and may draw blood from the knee to relieve the swelling and the pain. If the swelling is not so great get the player home *as soon as possible* and continue the cold and elevation treatment. If a long coach journey has to be made from an away match you can apply a cold compress to the knee in the bus.

1. Fold a small towel so that the breadth of the folded towel is about six inches.
2. Soak the towel in cold water.
3. Wrap it round the knee as often as it will go.
4. Wrap a three inch elastic bandage round the towel firmly but not tightly.

Fig. 24 Elevation of the lower limb by the insertion of a chair under the mattress.

When the player has reached home you may leave the towel on if the player finds it comfortable and it is possible to elevate the knee to a much greater height above the heart at home. The foot of the bed can be elevated on bricks, or a chair can be put under the mattress and this reduces the need for a compression bandage. The player should stay like this for at least twenty-four hours and may need aspirin or paracetamol for pain (see page 112). He can then start to walk again. At this point an elastic knee support is sometimes helpful — ask the advice of a pharmacist about knee-bandages. After the player has for at least a week been free from pain while walking he can resume gentle quadricep exercises and then gradually build up to match fitness (see page 88). If a ligament is completely torn the player will be in severe pain and will be unable to rise or continue playing. If the knee swells markedly and is painful the player should be taken to hospital the same day because the doctor may decide to draw blood from the knee to relieve the pain. Ligaments which have been completely torn can be repaired by an operation but this is not done at the time of the injury.

### Torn cartilages
The top surface of the tibia is flat. The bottom of the femur is round but not perfectly hemispherical. In some positions of the knee-joint a greater surface area of bone is in contact than in others. Because the area in contact varies, the pressure applied to the bone-ends will also vary and to reduce the effects of this there are two shock absorbers present in the knee. These are the cartilages, which also act as stabilizers. There are two cartilages — the medial (or inner)

and the lateral (or outer). Each is a crescent-shaped structure about the same consistency as the cartilage in your ear — feel your ear to get some idea of the nature of this cartilage. As the femur moves on the tibia the cartilages change position and shape to reduce the force of the femur on the tibia and so stabilize the joint. In so doing they are subjected to immense shearing forces and, if the femur changes its position quickly, either the medial cartilage or lateral cartilage may be trapped at the point of the greatest pressure and be torn. This usually happens when the player is pivoting on one foot with his knee bent, a very common position in football. It can occur as the result of a clash between two players, but this is uncommon. The player falls and has pain in the knee, which is usually more marked on the inner aspect of the knee. He may be unable to straighten the knee fully. If this has occurred the player should be taken off and elevation and cold treatment used to slow the rate of bleeding. If the knee 'locks', that is sticks when the player tries to straighten it, do not attempt to force it straight. The knee may straighten slowly overnight. If the player is in severe pain or if his leg is locked to a degree that makes it very difficult for him to get home he should be taken to hospital. If he is able to hobble to the team bus and is not in too much pain he can be allowed to go home if he will elevate his knee when he gets there by propping up the foot of his bed. The player will usually find that his knee improves over a couple of weeks. Early treatment of a ligament injury is important to help it heal. Cartilages cannot heal once they have been torn so, unless the player is in severe pain, or has a very swollen knee or the knee is locked he does not need to go to hospital immediately. He should apply the home treatment, using aspirin or paracetamol as necessary to control the pain, and make an appointment to see his own doctor.

If a player has torn a cartilage he is liable to be affected time after time and the only cure is to remove the cartilage. The knee can function quite well without it. Some older players may prefer to retire rather than have an operation but they are likely to suffer a recurrence while golfing, gardening, turning over in bed or performing any movement that involves rotation of the leg. The operation is simple and recovery is quick and the player can seek advice from the physiotherapist he meets in hospital about returning to train and to play. The advice he will be given is designed to strengthen his quadriceps or thigh muscles.

## Quadriceps rehabilitation

The thigh muscles or the quadriceps group of muscles — so called because they are in four distinct parts — are the most important factor in stabilising the knee. If the knee is immobilised for some weeks the quadriceps muscles waste (shrink) and it is essential to concentrate on strengthening them before the player returns to full training or to play in matches. Rehabilitation (see **page 12**) is particularly important.

If the knee has been severely damaged or the player has had an operation he may be fortunate enough to have the advice of a doctor, remedial gymnast or physiotherapist. If he has not this quality of advice available you and he will have to work out a programme of exercises.

The simplest form of quads exercises can be done in bed. Sit down on the floor now and try the following set of exercises:

1. Put your leg out straight in front of you.
2. Try to pull your foot back towards you as hard as you can. You will immediately feel the quadriceps muscle tense.
3. Push your leg, with the quadriceps tense holding the knee straight, down into the floor. You will feel the quadriceps tense even more tightly.
4. Lift the whole leg straight off the ground.

Many players believe that they can strengthen the quadriceps by straightening the knee with a weight attached to the foot while sitting on a bench or table. If you watch players exercise like this, however, you will observe that the great majority of them stop lifting the leg before the lower limb is completely straight. When there is a couple of degrees still to go they stop and let the leg flop down again; yet it is the last few degrees which are the most important because it is during this part of the act that the all important muscle fibres near the knee-cap contract. More effective exercise is for the player to stand, lean forward and hold on to a table of suitable height and, by raising the ankle, bend the knee which has been damaged. If the player now brings the heel down so that the foot is flat on the floor the knee will have to become straight and this action brings into play the important fibres. Try this yourself now. Give the player sets of this exercise to try. As the muscle gets stronger place your hand behind the knee and put some resistance against the movement while he repeats the exercise.

Next, encourage the player to exercise the quadriceps muscles by sitting on a bench and straightening the knee with a weight attached to the foot. The weight should not be greater than 1 kilo and may be made by tying sand in a plastic shopping bag. *However, this exercise is useless unless the knee is locked absolutely straight on each occasion.*

Swimming is also useful provided that racing dives and vigorous breast-stroke leg-kicks are avoided.

The final stage of rehabilitation is jogging, building up gradually to sprinting.

## KNEE STRAPPING

It is possible to strap a knee but all the reservations we have previously stated about strapping apply particularly to the knee. Strapping is no substitute for strong quadriceps muscles and should not be used to encourage a player to play who has not fully recovered from a knee injury although some players demand support for their knees even though they are perfectly fit. If you are able to learn how to strap a knee from someone who has been professionally trained take the opportunity to do so. It may come in useful, for example with the nervous player who always says that his knee should be supported. However, we believe that knee strapping is so difficult that it cannot be taught adequately by diagrams and drawings. The untrained manager or coach is better advised, in our opinion, to encourage the player to consult a pharmacist and buy a good elastic knee support than to attempt to strap the knee unskilfully.

## CHRONIC PAIN

Chronic pain in the knee of young players is always a problem which should be taken seriously. If someone who is not yet fully grown complains of recurrent or continuous pain behind the knee-cap, or in front of the shin bone at the point at which the patellar tendon is attached, or in any other place, an appointment should be made for him to see a doctor. This advice applies to chronic pain which occurs in other joints such as the hip or in the middle of a bone. It is not normal to have 'growing pains' — a doctor should be consulted if a growing youngster has pain in a bone or joint which is unrelated to an injury and lasts for a long time.

In older players chronic pain is not uncommon in or around the knee. It is the end result of years of wear and tear and there is no specific cure for it. If the pain becomes severe, if it troubles the player every match or training session, or if he is suffering from pain for hours after every match or is much more stiff on the morning after than he was formerly, he should make an appointment with his doctor. A player who is thirty-five may be making use of his knee-joints for forty, fifty or sixty years more and if he is showing signs and feeling symptoms of wear and tear he would be wise to consider retiring from playing and take up swimming or cycling, which are forms of exercise less damaging to the knees. He could also become a manager, trainer or coach and transfer the wear and tear from his knees to his nerves!

# 10.
# SHOULDERS AND HANDS

## SHOULDER INJURIES

The femur — the thigh bone — lies deeply in the pelvis and the weight of the body pressing on this ball and socket joint increases the joint's stability. In men and women the shoulder joint is much less stable than the hip joint although it is much more mobile. The humerus — the armbone — does not plug into the shoulder blade, as the femur plugs into the pelvis. Furthermore, the arm hangs from the body so that the whole weight must be supported by the muscles and tendons which surround the shoulder joint. Rest one hand on the most prominent part of the shoulder. Now lift the arm out horizontally and let it drop back to your side several times and feel the muscles which run from the shoulder blade behind the shoulder joint and the collar bone in front of it and down onto the humerus. These muscles and their tendons attach the arm to the body and preserve the stability of the shoulder joint itself. There are no stray ligaments round the shoulder joint, as there are round the ankle joint; even the fibrous sleeve of the joint is very weak.

**Acute pain**
Always follow the Golden Rule — Look and Listen before you Touch. Sit the player down, support his back and lay a blanket or rug over his legs to keep him warm. Allow him to take up the position which he finds most comfortable. He may hold his wrist, even though his shoulder has been injured, or support the elbow on the injured side with the other hand. Then ask him how the injury happened. Ask him to point exactly to the place at which the pain is greatest. Identify that point on the opposite uninjured shoulder and feel it first, trying to determine exactly what structure lies under the skin at that point. Stand a pace or two back and have a good look at an injured shoulder from a distance; if it has been dislocated you may not notice the difference if you peer too closely. If the pain is most severe near the shoulder joint itself the fibrous sleeve of the joint may be torn. If it is most severe on the collar bone it may be fractured. Put a triangular bandage on and take the player to see a doctor the same day if you suspect a dislocation or fracture. Don't attempt to reduce a dislocation yourself. If the doctor does not prescribe anything for the pain offer the player aspirin or paracetemol (see page 112) to take for the next twenty-four hours.

## Chronic pain

If a player develops pain every time he plays or trains he may be suffering from the cumulative effects of a number of minor injuries which have occurred on and around the shoulder joint over the years. The bones of the joint may have become roughened, the muscles may have sustained many minor tears and the fibrous capsule of the joint may also have many small scars from numerous minor injuries. The end result is sometimes called a frozen shoulder, that is a shoulder which is both painful and stiff. For chronic shoulder pain an appointment should be made with the player's doctor or with a physiotherapist because it requires careful treatment to prevent permanent stiffness.

## HAND INJURIES

The hand is commonly injured either by a kick or by the player landing his full weight on the hand or by being stood on. All types of injury are, of course, more common among goalkeepers.

The result of a kick may be a fracture. Look carefully at the point at which the player feels most pain, identify the point on the other hand and try to determine exactly what lies under the skin at that point. Give the injured hand an X-ray look — try to see exactly what is happening. Tenderness on or very near a bone indicates a possible fracture and the player should go to hospital the same day. If the hand is placed in a bucket of cold or iced water the pain will be reduced but it is very difficult to keep a bucket of iced water above the level of a player's heart while transporting him to hospital so you will have to elevate the hand in a sling.

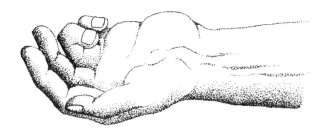

Fig. 25  Left hand lying in the resting position.

Lay your hand on the table. It naturally assumes a position with the fingers flexed, the little finger being the most flexed. This is the natural resting position and it is the best position in which to bind the hand. Place a pad and a rolled bandage in the hand and wrap it loosely in a broad bandage. Then support the bound hand in a triangular sling above the level of the heart. Try this now on a friend or member of your household.

This technique is also useful if the keeper is hit by a ball on the point of the fingers. With this sort of blow the result is usually damage to the ligaments of one or more of the small joints between the finger bones. Again the first aid treatment is to plunge the hand in a bucket of cold or iced water and then allow the player to let it fall into the resting position and bind it up in a sling in the way we have described. There is usually *no need* to take the player to hospital with this type of injury unless one of the joints is very deformed. Even if you have seen someone reduce a dislocated finger and thought that it looked easy, don't try to do it yourself. Take the player to hospital on the same day.

The player should keep his hand as high above the level of the heart as possible for forty-eight hours after the match. He should continue to move the fingers as much as is comfortable in the first forty-eight hours after the injury. After this time the bleeding from the torn blood vessels near the ligaments should have stopped; the player should start exercising the hand for five minutes at a time every two hours under hot water to prevent stiffness. If a keeper's hands become very stiff after years of playing he should consult a doctor or physiotherapist.

A fall on the hand may result in pain in the wrist or in the base of the forearm or around the elbow. If such pain occurs a fracture is possible and the player should be taken to hospital the same day. If the bones are obviously out of shape or if the player is in severe pain and he is only a youngster, take him to hospital *immediately*.

Put the forearm in a bucket of cold water then support it in a sling.

## DON'T FORGET THE GOALKEEPER

Shoulder and hand injuries are particularly prevalent among goal-keepers and this is an appropriate place to discuss their special needs.

There is an old football saying that goalkeepers are mad. We do not believe this but we do believe that goalkeepers are different from other players. They are at greater risk of injury and their needs are too often forgotten.

Goalkeepers are, in general, braver than other players and less likely to hold back. This increases the risk of injury in some situations but decreases it in others, because the player who goes in half-heartedly is often more at risk of injury. Goalkeepers are also less selfish than other players and will often expose themselves to risks for the good of the team.

If you do not have a goalkeeper on the coaching staff of your club try to find one who will help out. It doesn't matter how old he is. In fact the older the better because the goalkeepers, or goalies, of yesteryear were much less well protected from rumbustious centre forwards than their present day descendants. The most important thing to teach a goalkeeper is how to position himself. If he positions himself with care and is taught when to leave his goal line he can command the penalty area and will have to dive at the feet of a forward who is running in to a through ball or cross ball less often than the keeper who leaves his line too late to intercept the ball.

Notice how much space the good keeper always appears to have around him when he gathers the ball. All keepers, no matter how good, have to go to meet players advancing with the ball at their feet. Ensure that the keeper learns how to go down safely, keeping his head well away from the players' feet — goalkeepers have been killed diving headfirst at the feet of a forward. Teach the goalkeeper how to go in feet first with arms ready to parry a shot; it is better goalkeeping as well as being safer because the keeper presents a bigger obstacle to the advancing players. Skill training is as important for goalkeepers as for players in other positions. Plenty of practice in dealing with high crosses means that such balls will be caught cleanly rather than stubbing the keeper's fingers.

The development of good team work in the penalty area reduces the keeper's chance of being injured by his own players because they will get out of his way when he shouts 'mine' and goes for the ball. Many injuries take place in the six-yard box and it must be clearly established how players should react when the keeper takes command.

The keeper's kit is also important. If he can play in two jerseys rather than one he should do so and if he has never tried two jerseys he should do. A 'grass burn' or abrasion (see page 45) on a shoulder, elbow or hip will be made more comfortable and will be protected from further injury if a thick layer of vaseline is smeared on the sensitive area. Long trousers of some sort should be worn much more often than they are at present. When the ground is hard they are obviously protective but when it is soft they are also protective because of the common practice of putting sand on soft goal areas. A keeper who does not wish to wear long trousers, and some just do not feel they can move easily in them, should be advised to wear shorts which are as long as possible and knee bandages not to support the ligaments of the knee but to protect the skin. Gloves protect the skin as well as helping the keeper deal with a wet ball.

This advice is particularly important for boys' teams. It is more common in boys' football to switch players from one position to another so that a boy who was kitted out to play on the left wing may find himself shivering and unprotected on the goal line after half-time. There should always be spare kit so that a person who 'pulls on the injured keeper's jersey', as the Press say, can be adequately protected. There should be a spare jersey because the keeper who has injured a shoulder may find it impossible to take his jersey off.

Goalkeepers also require a more elaborate warming up programme because they place many more muscles under severe strain than other players do. Shoulder muscles, neck muscles, those surrounding the spinal column and those of the abdominal wall must all be loosened. You and the keeper will be able to work at a series of exercises to loosen off all these muscles using the principles set out in the chapter on muscle injuries (Chapter 7). Briefly these are:

1. Select the muscles which you wish to loosen off.
2. Adopt a position which extends these muscles to their comfortable limit.
3. Then, very *slowly* and *gently*, move so that the muscles are stretched just that little bit more.

For example, to loosen off the back muscles, read then practice this sequence of movements. Stand up, place your feet apart, bend forward, keeping your knees straight, and let your body drop slowly and gently until it can go no further. Then, *very slowly and very gently*, just push your hands through between your legs until you feel the strain on the back muscles. Now lay the book down, stand up and do it again. Work out for yourself ways of loosening off all the muscles of the neck, abdominal wall, spinal column and shoulders.

# 11.
# VULNERABLE AREAS

## Brain damage

Take a clear glass. Pour about one inch of rice grains into it and then pour about an inch of lentils on top. The two layers are clearly distinguished. Now jerk the glass sideways for about six inches and then reverse the direction of movement suddenly, taking care not to spill any of the contents. Now observe the contents and you will see that the arrangement of grains has been disturbed. Repeat this ten times and see how much the original layers have been shaken up. Even though the cells of the brain are more firmly embedded than the rice and lentils which you have used they too are affected by rapid acceleration and deceleration and a blow to the head may cause unconsciousness in the same way. Often a blow from the ball or ground does not have a direct effect on the bit of the brain immediately below the part of the skull at which the contact took place. It is the sudden deceleration of the whole head, and therefore the whole brain, which is important. All the nerve cells are affected and the player loses consciousness. This type of diffuse brain damage was called 'concussion' but this term is not used so much by doctors nowadays.

If the blow to the skull is from a hard object, such as a boot or a goalpost, the skull may fracture at the point of contact and the part of the brain immediately under that area of skull may be damaged. If you were to drive a nail through the side of the glass you would obviously disturb the rice and lentils underneath the broken glass and a fracture of the skull can cause damage in the same way. In this type of injury consciousness may not be lost even though a part of the player's brain has been damaged. Sometimes both types of brain damage occur together.

Some situations require the player to be taken to hospital *as soon as possible*:

    1. If unconsciousness persists and the player shows no sign of recovery of consciousness for five minutes. ANY PLAYER WHO BECOMES UNCONSCIOUS SHOULD BE ROLLED ONTO HIS FRONT IMMEDIATELY. Obviously he should not be laid flat on his face but placed in what is called the Recovery Position. Practice this now on your wife, girlfriend or anyone else who is available.

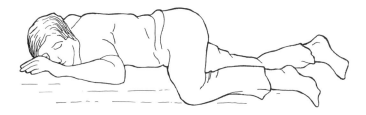

Fig. 26 The Recovery position.

2. If clear fluid runs from the player's nose or ears, either alone or mixed with blood.
3. If he has difficulty in seeing or in moving an arm or leg.
4. If he has sustained a deep cut on the scalp as the result of a blow. A scalp wound which results from a glancing blow should be treated like any other cut — sit the player upright and apply cold and pressure. If however, a scalp wound has been caused by a direct blow to the head from a post or boot there is a possibility that the blow may also have caused a fracture in the bone underneath the cut.
5. If the player becomes unconscious some time after he has sustained the blow to the head. Occasionally a player who had apparently suffered only a minor injury begins to vomit and to be drowsy in the dressing room or at home after a game.

If any of these problems occur the player should be taken to hospital *as soon as possible*. These decisions are relatively easy to make although the situations in which they arise are obviously serious and can be very worrying. It is, surprisingly, much more difficult to decide if a player should be taken to hospital when the head injury is not serious. Everyone would agree that a player who remains unconscious for half an hour should go to hospital, but what about the player who is unconscious for half a minute? In our opinion any player who has been unconscious should not play again in that match even if he appears to recover quickly. He should be taken off and should not be allowed to return alone to the dressing room. At the end of the game, or at half-time if the player is injured in the first half, ask the player if he can remember what happened *after* the injury. If he cannot remember everything which happened *since* the injury he should be taken to hospital *as soon as possible* even though he is able to carry on an intelligent conversation. You should do your best to discourage any player who has sustained a head injury, no matter how minor, from drinking *any* alcohol that evening. He should also be rested from matches for three weeks — even though he has only been unconscious for a few seconds — although he can train, provided he does not head the ball.

## Blows to the face and nose

Black eyes result from bleeding into the soft tissues round the eyeball. If the player sits upright and presses a cold pad to the area bleeding will be minimised. A raw steak, the traditional remedy for a black eye, is no more effective and is very much more expensive than a cold sponge. If the player has a spot of pain on one of the bones around the eye, either above it or on the cheek bones, a fracture should be suspected and the player should be taken to hospital *as soon as possible*.

Bleeding from the nose is common and can be simply treated. Tell the player to squeeze the soft part of the nose between finger and thumb and breathe through his mouth for ten minutes. If the bleeding does not stop continue for twenty minutes longer, then take the player to hospital if the bleeding persists. If you or the player thinks that the nose is actually broken there is no need to take him to hospital that same day, provided you can stop the bleeding. Give the player aspirin and paracetamol if he is in pain (see page 112) and tell him to make an appointment to see his own doctor. Immediate diagnosis and treatment is not essential for a broken nose.

If a player has pain which persists after the game in any part of his face such as his cheek or jaw, he may have fractured a facial bone and should go to hospital *as soon as possible*.

## Mouth injuries

This section should be consulted in conjunction with the section on dentists (see page 20). Two types of mouth injury are common:

1. A direct blow to the front of the mouth from another player's head or elbow or from the ball.
2. A blow on the under side of the chin which brings the lower set of teeth sharply in contact with the upper, sometimes trapping the tongue. This may result from an uppercut but more usually occurs when a player who has gone for a high ball comes down on top of another player's head.

*Frontal blows*

A direct blow to the front of the mouth can cause cuts on the inside of the lips or broken teeth or a tooth can be knocked out completely. The first point to emphasise is that such injuries are preventable. If the player is wearing a mouthguard or gumshield the force of the blow is absorbed in the soft material of the mouthguard. It is possible to buy mouthguards in most sports shops, and these are better than no protection but they are not as good as the mouthguard which has been made to measure by a dentist. For schoolboys who are growing quickly the sports shop mouthguards are usually preferable because they are cheaper.

Mouthguards are not available on the NHS so the player has to make an appointment with his dentist and be prepared to pay for the mouthguard. The dentist will take an impression of the player's mouth and arrange for the guard to be made by a dental technician. A properly-fitting mouthguard is more comfortable and much more effective in protecting teeth.

It is unnecessary for every player to wear a mouthguard but the type of player who is prepared to go for every ball should be encouraged to protect his mouth. So, too, should players who have had expensive dental work, such as a crown, done or, in the case of boys, orthodontic braces inserted.

If the lips are cut on the inside they bleed profusely and swell up alarmingly because the tissue round the mouth is richly supplied with blood vessels. The application of a sterile pad soaked in cold water should stop the bleeding quickly. Such cuts may look as though they need stitches because they often gape widely open after the bleeding has stopped but there is often no need to take the player to a doctor. Cuts inside the lips hardly ever become infected and usually heal without needing stitches. If you cannot stop the bleeding by the use of pressure the player should be seen by a doctor *as soon as possible*. The other time when you should consult a doctor about a mouth or tooth injury is when the bone of the upper or lower jaw feels painful above a broken tooth or close to a cut on the inside of the lip. Persistent pain in the bones of the face means that a fracture is a possibility, as persistent pain of any bone means that a fracture should be suspected and the player should be taken to hospital the same day.

*Uppercuts*

If the upper and lower teeth are brought sharply together teeth can be broken, unless the tongue is in the way in which case it acts as a shock-absorber, being cut in the process. Cuts on the tongue, like those on the inside of the lips, bleed profusely but heal well. Unless the tip of the tongue is actually hanging off the cut should be treated like any other. Press a cold sterile pad to the cut area and hold it there for ten minutes. If there is pain in the jawbone there may be a fracture and the player should be taken to hospital *as soon as possible*. This is usually easy to diagnose because the player is in great pain and the jaw is hanging loosely. Tie a bandage gently but firmly under the jaw and round the head to support the jaw.

## Dental Problems
*Broken teeth*. If you can see a pink or red spot on the tooth where a part has broken off, the nerve is exposed and the player should see a dentist *as soon as possible*, so that infection can be prevented. If the player has been knocked out and has had teeth broken he should be taken to hospital *as soon as possible* because he may have swallowed a part of a tooth (collect up any bits of tooth and take them to hospital; it helps the doctor to decide whether or not it is likely that a bit has been swallowed).

*Avulsed teeth*. Occasionally a tooth or teeth are knocked cleanly out of the jaw. If you suspect that a fracture is present clean the tooth, and slip it into the mouth between cheek and teeth and take him to hospital *as soon as possible*. If there is no fracture clean the tooth and try to put it back in the socket; make sure it is facing the right way. Then take the player to a dentist *as soon as possible*. The tooth socket is numb immediately after a tooth has been knocked out. If there is any pain or difficulty ask the player to keep the tooth in his cheek, to keep it bathed in body fluid and take the player to a dentist *as soon as possible*. If the player is unconscious do not put a tooth or a bit of tooth back in the mouth.

## Eye injuries
### Dirt and mud
This is the most common type of problem. When a player gets dirt or mud in his eye do not try to wipe it out. The best first aid measure is to take the player to the nearest tap and allow him to splash water on his eye with his hand. NEVER ADD ANTISEPTIC TO WATER USED ON THE EYE. If you are in any doubt whether you have removed all the dirt or if the player continues to complain of pain or irritation although you cannot see any more dirt he should be taken to the nearest hospital. Give him a sterile pad to

hold to his eye for the trip to hospital. This is a useful piece of equipment to carry in your first aid kit.

## Cuts

Cuts which occur around the eye, on the eyebrows for example, should be managed like any other cut except that ANTISEPTIC MUST BE USED WITH GREAT CAUTION NEAR THE EYE. If the cut affects an eyelid or if the eyeball itself is thought to have been damaged the player should be given an eye pad to put on and he should be taken to hospital.

## Disturbance or loss of vision

It is common for vision to be affected after a blow to the head or the eye — 'seeing stars'. It is, however, not normal for double vision to continue and if any player who has had a head injury or a direct blow to the eye complains of double vision he should be taken to hospital *as soon as possible* even though he did not lose consciousness. Similarly, a player who complains that he cannot see clearly out of one eye should be taken to hospital *as soon as possible* even if he cannot recall having any knock to his eye or in the region of his eye.

## Contact lenses

Players who wear spectacles can wear contact lenses while playing. Either the small hard or the large soft type of lenses can be worn. The main risk with the former type is that they are more easily knocked out and lost. The search for good players is often very frustrating but it is easy in comparison with the search for a contact lens on a muddy pitch. A player who wishes to wear contact lenses should consult an optician.

## BREAST INJURIES

In general, women footballers sustain the same type of injuries as men. In many ways women are more resilient than men and many women bear pain with greater fortitude, but their breasts are more vulnerable than the scanty breast tissue which lies underneath the male nipple. Running imposes a strain on breast tissue. Some women have enough elastic tissue in their breasts to train and play a game without discomfort but others require a bra. The bra not only protects against painful breasts, it helps protect the nipples. The nipple of a woman moves much more than the nipple of a man during running and the female nipple may be rubbed by a loose jersey so that it becomes painful. A well fitting bra can also prevent painful nipples. Direct blows to the breasts are, of course, painful but the pain can be minimised if a cold sponge is pressed to the breast and held there for at least ten minutes because it slows down the bleeding which results from the blow and causes some of the pain.

Although women are vulnerable in this way, their genital organs — the ovaries — are safely buried in the abdominal cavity.

## TESTICULAR INJURIES

The genital organs of men — the testicles — are suspended in a very vulnerable position. A kick in the testicles is sickeningly painful, and the pain courses through the body to the kidney region. Unfortunately little can be done to relieve the acute pain. Fortunately it soon passes but if a player still has pain in a testicle at the end of the match it is wise to consult a doctor *as soon as possible*. It can happen that a player develops pain in a testicle while training or playing even though he has not been kicked or struck by a ball. This type of problem should be taken to a doctor *as soon as possible*. If the player has pain on passing urine or passes blood in his urine after a kick in the testicles, the crutch or the back he should see a doctor the same day.

If the testicles are supported instead of hanging free the risk of injury is reduced but the supporting garment should not be too tight. If it is, the testicles may be at greater risk because they are trapped against the bone of the pelvis when struck. For this reason loose swimming trunks are sometimes safer than very tight fitting supports or jock-straps. The jock-strap has one advantage over swimming trunks — it presses firmly on the weak point of the abdominal wall and reduces the risk of a hernia or rupture developing. Whatever is worn, whether jock-strap or swimming trunks, it should be washed as often as the player's socks, that is, it should be washed every time it is worn. If it is not the player can develop a nasty skin infection in the groin for which he should make an appointment to see his doctor.

Finally, remember that, even though some of the pain in testicular injuries results from bleeding into the tissue of the testicle, players will not thank you for employing the usual means of controlling bleeding, namely the elevation of the injured part above the level of the heart and the application of an ice-pack and pressure!

## Abdominal Pain

It is extremely rare for a player hit on the abdomen with a football to suffer serious injury. He will usually recover quickly from the winding. If, however, he is kicked the damage may be more serious. Apply an ice-pack to the area which has been kicked and hold it there until the pain goes. Bleeding into the muscles of the abdominal wall can be very painful. If the player becomes shocked, that is becomes very pale and either faints or vomits blood after being kicked, he should be taken to hospital *as soon as possible*.

## Chest Pain

A player who is kicked or elbowed in the chest or ribs may suffer a rib fracture. A broken rib should be suspected when a player can indicate on a rib, or ribs, exactly where he feels a sharp pain on breathing in or out. If a fracture is suspected he should be taken to hospital *as soon as possible*. There the medical staff will exclude the possibility of damage to the lung but they will not strap the chest as it is now appreciated that it is best for the lungs and chest not to be constricted by tight strapping.

A player who develops a severe pain in his chest, neck or left arm while he is playing or training may be having a heart attack. It is common to feel pain or discomfort when running in cold air — we are all familiar with that feeling. The pain of a heart attack is completely different, and is commonly described as 'crushing' or 'like tightening steel bands' or 'choking'. It is sometimes accompanied by breathlessness and faintness and the person may sweat heavily and turn very pale or bluish. If a heart attack is suspected the person — player, referee, spectator or linesman — affected should immediately cease all activity and must be taken to hospital *as soon as possible*.

# 12.
# PRE-MATCH PREPARATION

## Late nights

No one is certain what physical changes cause tiredness, either the tiredness which occurs the day after a match or that which occurs after a late or broken night. Because no one knows the physical cause of tiredness, it is impossible to cure it by physical means although much can be done to 'lift' a tired player by psychological means. There is little evidence that sugar — whether it is given as honey, glucose, sucrose, or any other form — banishes tiredness but if the player *believes* that it does he will probably be helped. As cure is impossible, the emphasis must be on the prevention of tiredness, that is on the 'prevention' of late nights and sleeplessness.

Managers of professional players are in a position to command their players to stay at home and go to bed early. Some even take their squad to a hotel so that they can be sure their instructions are followed. But few managers take this approach. They know that they are working with mature people, for the most part, and prefer to try to make the players see the wisdom of early nights rather than impose them. Besides they know that one or two players might take a command to stay in as a challenge to go out and that no one can sleep to order. Managers of amateur teams do not have this authority and they must try to educate their players or, to be more accurate, to encourage them to be sensible, because everyone knows that late nights are tiring.

The effects of a late night can be minimised if the player has a long lie-in the following morning. This does not mean that players should be allowed to use the excuse that they can have a long lie-in to justify late nights. It does mean, however, that if a player wishes to have a late night for a good reason, for example, a special birthday party, he can be advised to stay in bed until eleven the next morning. Of course, in teams in which the players are not taking the game too seriously it may be impossible to influence the behaviour of players at all. They may protest that they are only playing 'for fun' but the manager or coach's answer to this is simple. If players are going to treat the matches so casually that they are not prepared to make any sacrifice for them then the coach or manager need make no sacrifice either. There is little point in giving up your evening to coach or train a team whose members take to the pitch like zombies every match-day.

## Hangovers

The physical factors which produce the symptoms of a hangover are not precisely known either. The chemicals in an alcoholic drink which are called congeners and give it its flavour — alcohol itself is tasteless — give rise to some of the effects. For this reason brandy, which contains a higher concentration of these chemicals than vodka tends to cause a worse hangover. However, the alcohol itself causes some of the symptoms and a hangover will therefore result whatever type of alcoholic drink has been consumed. Alcohol has two important effects: it causes dehydration due to an excessive passage of water in the urine, and it causes the blood–glucose concentration to drop to a level which causes the person to feel unwell.

The best strategy for dealing with hangovers is, of course, prevention but if a player is going to have a few drinks he should be encouraged to drink a pint of water before he goes to bed, and to drink a glass of water every time he wakes to go to the toilet during the night. He should also drink at least half a pint of water as soon as he gets up in the morning. He should also have hot *sweet* tea to correct the low blood glucose level. If he has a stomach ache, or feels sick he should take some dry bread or water biscuits and if he has a headache he can take paracetamol (see page 112) — not aspirin as it can irritate the stomach lining, which is sensitive after heavy drinking.

Some events which fall on the nights before a match, such as a wedding or anniversary party, are excusable causes of hangovers but players who repeatedly report for play with a hangover are not only reducing the team's chance of winning and their team mates' enjoyment but also making the time you have sacrificed for that player a waste of time; such players should be told so. Players have the *right* to go out and get drunk but they also have *obligations* to their team mates and to you.

## Sleeplessness

Even if a player goes to bed early he may not sleep. In fact if he tries to go to bed two hours before his usual time of retiring he may toss and turn and become so restless that he does not drop off until long after his usual time of sleeping. It is helpful to advise nervous players to go to bed at the same time as usual unless, of course, they feel tired and ready for sleep earlier. Also, they should try and follow the same routine every Friday night. A light meal — rich and fatty foods should be avoided by all players on a Friday night — an hour watching television, a warm bath, and a cup of warm milk or a small amount of an alcoholic drink before retiring induces the right frame of mind for sleep, especially if it is followed so regularly that it becomes a ritual. Sleeping pills are not advisable the night before a game as they may still be having an effect when you want the player to be at his most wide awake.

## Sex
There is no evidence that sex affects a player's performance. Even if there were, there would be little point in trying to dissuade players from sex for the good of the team, although this is probably partly the reason why professionals are taken away to a hotel for a night or two before a match.

SATURDAY MORNING

## Pre-match nutrition
The concentration of glucose in the blood begins to increase about forty minutes after a meal because it takes that time for the glucose to filter across the intestinal wall, unlike a petrol gauge which shows the energy input immediately. After increasing to a concentration about twice that which was present before the meal the level then falls slowly until the next meal, just as the petrol gauge falls slowly as the car uses up fuel. Unlike a motor car, the blood is never without glucose because the body reacts when the concentration falls below a certain level. It then mobilises glucose from the liver — the body's reserve tank — until the next meal has been consumed, digested and absorbed. It would not, however, be wise to have a meal forty minutes before kick-off. Although it would be best from the point of view of the blood glucose concentration, it would be unwise because few players can play with a full stomach. It takes a few hours for the stomach to empty its contents into the small intestine and until this has happened a person who takes vigorous exercise is liable to feel nauseated or to vomit. The last meal should, therefore, be taken between two and three hours before kick-off. It should be light in weight but rich in energy and it is prudent to avoid fatty foods because fats remain in the stomach much longer than other types of food.

A sensible energy plan for an afternoon match is to have a substantial breakfast — for example, cereals, toast (preferably wholemeal) and an egg with coffee or tea — about nine o'clock with a light, energy-rich meal just after noon. If the player wants protein he can be offered grilled fish or chicken which is more digestible than red meat, and he should not consume large helpings of vegetables. It must be emphasised that there is no need to have protein at this pre-match meal and players do just as well on honey sandwiches as on fish, and will do better on honey sandwiches than on steak! (Remember that the great tradition for pre-match steak was probably influenced by the fact that many footballers in the nineteen twenties and thirties seized any opportunity to eat meat with alacrity and always chose meat before a match for the simple reason that someone else was paying for it). The player can be offered a light sweet at the end of the mid-day meal but a chocolate biscuit is as effective — *Always encourage the players to clean their teeth when they are on a high sugar diet.* Carry a few new toothbrushes with you and a tube of toothpaste.

Make sure you have some biscuits in the dressing room. A digestive biscuit or water biscuit in the dressing room can help a nervous player because it mops up the acid which may be swilling about in his empty stomach and it reassures him that he will have enough energy to see him through the game.

Every player is different and most will have worked out their own satisfactory routine. This is a good subject to discuss during a training session. Some players have very strange eating habits which should be corrected, for example some fast the whole day before a match, while others have habits which are unusual but acceptable because the player believes in them.

## Half-time and extra time

If a player has prepared himself for a match he has no need for extra sugar at half-time. Many professionals are offered, and consume sweet tea or a sweet lemon drink but managers of teams which have to huddle together at half time on the rainswept Gasworks ground should not be concerned because they cannot provide such hot sweet drinks. They do not make a significant contribution to the player's energy balance. If you need convincing, think of the second-half performance of players in rugby internationals, for they have to stand outside and usually do no more than suck an orange at half time. However, if a player has been used to taking some form of sugar at half-time and believes it does him good encourage him to continue. In the same way, it is often useful to offer players glucose or dextrose tablets before the start of extra time. They may receive some physical benefit, although it can take up to thirty minutes for the sugar to be absorbed, and they may receive a psychological boost, provided that you are confident when you give them the dextrose. Don't just hand out the tablets saying 'try one of these'; be confident and state emphatically 'now take this quick release form of energy, it will lift you for extra time'. Never force it on players. If a player says he doesn't want anything don't argue — he knows best.

## Fitness tests

At least one player is usually reported as receiving a 'final fitness test' on the Saturday morning sports programmes. Sometimes it is said to be a 'last minute fitness test'. We believe that such tests are appropriate only where the stakes are high, that is in professional football. For most managers a safe rule is that if the player's condition is such that his ability to play is in doubt on Saturday morning it should be accepted there and then that he is *not* fit to play a match on Saturday afternoon.

Even the most rigorous fitness test fails to impose the strain on a player's joints or muscles which will be imposed during a game. No matter how hard the player is made to work or how much he pushes himself, his injury is always in his mind during the fitness test and he always holds himself back just that little bit. When the manager shouts that he should change direction, for example, he may appear to do so immediately but he guards and protects the injured part while he does so. In the heat of the match with the ball at his feet, an opponent to his right and the goal to his left his reactions are different. Concentrating hard on the opportunity for a shot at goal and really fired up, all thoughts of his injury are banished from his mind and he pivots and shoots with every bit of force he can muster. The injury recurs even though he had passed his fitness test.

In all except the most important matches therefore, the rule is that, if in doubt on the morning, the decision should be to rest the player. An exception can be made if the match is very important to the player, not just because he wants to keep his place in the team but because it is a once in a lifetime opportunity, for example, a cup final or, in the case of a youngster a cap. His parents should be made fully aware of the possible consequences of playing. Exceptions are often made when the match is important to the club and here the manager's position is different. He must think of the player's well being, and, in our opinion, should not play someone whose fitness is suspect for the good of the team or the club.

# PREPARATION FOR INJURY

## THE TREATMENT ROOM

Those who belong to clubs which have their own clubhouse should start to scheme for a room in which all the necessary equipment can be stored. Those in smaller clubs who cannot hope to have a room devoted solely to the treatment of injuries should still try to ensure that they have all the major pieces of equipment and have a cupboard with a lock on it in which they can store supplies. Those heroes who take teams to pitches miles from any building, or who have to change and play in wooden sheds, concrete garages, or behind corrugated iron shacks will have to rely on the contents of their treatment bag, which we will describe in the next section.

1. Hot and cold running water is very useful.
2. A couch or table for the players to lie down in comfort, preferably propped up, allows for easy examination of injuries and treatment is easier to apply. If your club can afford the type of couch found in hospitals, which have a back rest that can be raised and lowered, you should agitate until they buy one.
3. A stretcher is needed infrequently but is the ideal way of carrying off an injured player; ask at your local Red Cross, St. John or St. Andrew's branch (see page 17) how to make one and attend one of their courses so that you can gain more experience of the types of injury which are stretcher cases.
4. Inflatable splints should be in every clubhouse. Medisport market the Medisport Wessex inflatable splint. Make sure you know how to use a splint *before* you are faced with a broken ankle.

Unless a trained physiotherapist or remedial gymnast is on the staff it is a waste of time, money and space to have any more elaborate equipment in the treatment room than these items.

## THE TREATMENT BAG

If you are playing at home and can take a player into the treatment room as soon as he is taken off, you only need a small number of items in your bag on the touchline. If you are playing away at a hospitable club with good facilities you need only take a limited range of items for treatment of injury. If, however, you are uncertain what facilities exist or want to be independent or know that there are no facilities at the ground you are visiting, you will have to take a well-stocked bag with you. Medisport makes two types of pre-packed cases, the Club Case and the more elaborate Pro Case, which is really designed for the coach with more detailed knowledge than the average reader of this book. Medisport also produces a compact touchline bag. Sportsystems also supply a case which is well designed and well-stocked to deal with most football injuries. Some trainers like this approach; others prefer to buy a bag with a zip, or a case, and prepare their own range of items. There is great scope for individuality because it is impossible to lay down hard and fast rules about what is best, with a few exceptions. It is up to the individual coach, trainer or manager to experiment, to exchange ideas with other coaches and trainers and to build on and review his own experience so that he assembles a treatment bag which suits his skills and the level of his knowledge. He also has to think of how much weight he can carry. Be careful not to take too much in the treatment bag. Not only can too much equipment confuse you in a crisis but you could suffer a hernia trying to run on to the field with a massive treatment bag. However, every bag should contain the following, or something similar to them:

1. A sponge, preferably a natural sponge.
2. A pack of sterile dressings and a pack of sterile cotton wool.
3. A pair of scissors with your name on them. People have no morals where scissors are concerned so it may be necessary to fix them to the bag with a long chain.
4. A pair of tweezers.
5. A large tin of talcum powder to put on parts of the skin which are nearly raw, for example between toes.
6. A large jar of vaseline for players who wish to protect cuts or grass burns. Smith and Nephew Ltd. make an aerosol spray called Op-site which sprays a strong protective film on cuts in awkward places, for example those on the jaw bone. If a player has a large grass burn which you wish to cover, Melolin or Jelonet non-adherent dressings, made by Smith and Nephew Ltd. are useful because they do not stick.
7. A small jar of Vick for players who feel they can't breathe properly because of a cold in the nose — a common problem in winter, or in hay fever time.
8. A triangular bandage.

9. At least two broad crepe bandages for holding sterile pads on cuts. The Medisport conforming elastic bandage is very useful because it is easy to apply as a safe pressure bandage. You should also pack a couple of small hand towels for this purpose (see page 12). It is useful to try a range of bandages because some people prefer the traditional style of cotton bandages; others prefer the bandages made with new materials, such as the Medilastic absorbent polyurethane bandage. We think these new materials are better than the traditional bandages for many purposes.

10. A selection of small adhesive plasters.

11. Adhesive strips for wound closure e.g. "Butterfly" strips.

12. Adhesive tapes, some broad, some narrow. Remember that some players are allergic to ordinary tape and need the special, more expensive, type of tape developed for such people. Hypal made by Smith and Nephew Ltd. is suitable for the purpose.

13. A packet of sterile eye patches.

14. The means of cooling an injured part. We emphasise the importance of cooling an injured part, to constrict the blood vessels and slow down the rate of bleeding, in the chapter on skin wounds. Ice can be applied to many injured parts but for some parts of the body it is better to immerse the whole part in very cold water. For example, an injured ankle can often be cooled most effectively by immersing the whole foot, boot and all if necessary, in a bucket. If the pain is localised, direct application of ice in some form or another is, however, more beneficial. Ice cubes or, better, crushed ice can be taken to a match in a thermos flask and applied to the injured area in a polythene bag or plastic sponge bag. It is also possible to buy ice-packs. These are plastic sachets which contain two chemicals in separate compartments. When they mix the temperature drops quickly. Medi-Ice sachets manufactured by Medisport are a very convenient way of carrying the means of cooling. Remember that ice can damage the skin and should not be applied for too long. Ice is certainly colder than water but cold water, whether in the magic sponge or in a bucket, has the advantage that the player can bear it for longer than he can bear an ice application. A two pound bag of frozen peas wrapped in a damp towel makes an excellent ice-pack because it can really be moulded to the injured part, but it is rather expensive unless

a suitable use can be found for the thawing peas — perhaps for your opponents' post match meal.
15. Aspirin and paracetamol.
16. A bottle of hydrogen peroxide solution.

The trainer should also take:
1. A bucket preferably with a lid.
2. A towel.
3. A blanket.
4. A packet of biscuits to kill 'butterflies' (see page 29).
5. Toothpaste, if travelling with a boys' team (see page 107).
6. An unbreakable water bottle.

Don't encourage players to chew gum when playing. A blow in the back and the chewing gum can go down the wrong way into the lungs.

Finally don't forget your own health. Don't get cold and wet. Keep warm and try not to smoke too many cigarettes during the game.

## ASPIRIN AND PARACETAMOL

We regard these drugs as two very important items in the treatment bag. Learn how to use them safely and you will able to relieve the pain of cuts, abrasions, pulled muscles, torn ligaments, and fractures. Pain has its uses. It warns the person that something is wrong and it is a warning which should not be ignored. (See page 74). This does not mean that pain should be left untreated. The measures we suggest for the management of each type of injury, for example, elevation of an injured ankle and the application of cold to the most painful area, will relieve some of the pain but frequently the person is left with pain even after they have received the correct treatment. It is then that aspirin and paracetamol can help. ASPIRIN AND PARACETAMOL SHOULD NOT BE USED BEFORE A MATCH. If a player needs painkillers before taking the pitch he is not fit to play.

Aspirin comes in many different forms. We recommend that you buy Soluble Aspirin B.P.; ask the pharmacist (see page 22) if you cannot see it in the pharmacy. Instruct the player to take two tablets dissolved in half a glass of water every few hours. He should be told that if he feels nausea or sickness or if he gets a buzzing noise in his ears he should stop taking aspirin. These side-effects are not serious but they provide a warning which should not be ignored. If they do occur, the player can take paracetamol which is the painkiller of first choice for people who suffer from indigestion frequently and for people who have or have had a stomach or duodenal ulcer.

Paracetamol is free from side-effects and is also an excellent painkiller. Some people prefer aspirin, or have more faith in aspirin, so keep both in your bag. As with aspirin there are a number of commercial preparations available but we again recommend the standard preparation, Paracetamol Tablets B.P. Instruct the player in pain to take two tablets every four or six hours up to a maximum of eight tablets a day.

Do not instruct boys to take aspirin or paracetamol; leave that to their parents. However, it is wise to suggest to the parents of a boy in pain that he may benefit from one of these drugs. They can then use one of the special children's preparations of aspirin or paracetamol if they wish. If you manage a boys team, keep some Paediatric Elixir BPC and some Paediatric Soluble Aspirin Tablets BPC in your bag because some parents will not have them in the house.

## SUPPLIERS

Three of the major suppliers are Smith and Nephew Ltd. and Medisport and Sportsystems.

Smith and Nephew Ltd.
Bessemer Road
Welwyn Garden City
Hertfordshire
AL7 1HF

Sportsystems
5 High Street
Windsor
Berks.

Medisport
Freepost
Ottershaw
Chertsey
Surrey KT16 OBR

They will send catalogues. Remember that your local pharmacist (see page 22) is an extremely valuable adviser. He knows a great deal about the various preparations and can advise you on what he thinks most suitable for your needs and your funds.

NEWMAN UNIVERSITY COLLEGE LIBRARY

# FINAL WHISTLE

The final whistle marks the end of the game for players and specta-tors. It marks the beginning of activity for the person responsible for the management of injury. In the same way we hope that the end of this book will mark the beginning of further activity on your part. We have emphasised on a number of occasions the importance of attending a first aid course run by the British Red Cross Society or the St John or, in Scotland, St Andrew's Ambulance Associa-tion, and of trying to help your local Football Association organise a course in the Basic Treatment of Injury leading to the Football Association Treatment of Injury Certificate. The regional coaches of the Football Association are excellent sources of advice on such courses.

For those who want to further their knowledge there are a number of excellent books which consider the subject in much greater depth that we have done; one is *Sports Injuries and Their Treatment* by J.H.C. Colson and W.J. Armour. However, such books are best read as part of a course of continuing education. The Football Association organises a three year course leading to the Association's Certificate in the Treatment and Rehabilitation of Injured Players, which is the ideal form of continuing education. This is a much more rigorous and academic course, which requires the student to study and to sit examinations. It is an excellent course for those wishing to study the subject in depth.

Those readers who have been very interested may wish to under-take full-time education to become a physiotherapist or a remedial gymnast. Entrance to the training courses depends in part upon the applicant's academic ability and qualifications because the training is demanding, but both professions offer interesting and rewarding jobs dealing with people who are injured and disabled — not only, of course, those disabled as a result of football injuries. Details about the necessary entrance qualifications and other information can be obtained from the Secretary of the Society of Remedial Gymnasts, Northampton Town Football Club, and from the Secretary of the Chartered Society of Physiotherapists, 14 Bedford Row, London WC1R 4ED. If, however, you do no more than remember the Golden Rules as a result of reading this book we will be satisfied. Play it Safe, Play it Cool, Look and Listen before you Touch, Prevention is better than Cure.

# INDEX

Abdomen, pain in, 103
Abrasions (grassburns), 40, 45
Achilles tendon, 47, 72; injuries, 50, 68; rehabilitation, 13
Adductor strains, 57
Allergy to sticking plaster, 15
Ankle injuries, 71–80; cuts on, 40; strapping, 76; twists, 73
Antibiotics, 42
Antiseptics, 42
Arches, fallen, 68
Aspirin, 112
Athlete's Foot, 65

Bacterial infection of skin wounds, 41
Black eyes, 107
Bleeding cuts, 10, 41
Blisters, 64
Breast injuries, 101
British Red Cross Society, 17, 23, 115
Bunion, 69
Butterflies, 29

Calf muscles, cramp, 59; loosening up 55; exercise,
Cartilage trouble, 86
Chest pain, 103
Chiropodists, 18, 60
Chiropractors, 21
Cigarette smoking, 33
Concussion, 96
Contusion (dead leg), 61
Corns, 66
Cramp, 59

Dead leg (contusion), 61
Dentists, 20, 99
Dextrose tablets, 29, 107
Diet, 29, 106
Doctors, 22

Eye injuries, 100

Fibula, 71
Fitness, 25–38; muscle, 26–7; heart-lung, 27–37, tests, 108
Fitness training for boys, 37
Foot problems, 63–70; prevention of, 63; cramp, 61
Football Association, treatment of injury courses, 3, 23, 115
Fractures, ankle (Pott's), 77; leg, 79; nose, 91; toe, 63; kneecap, 85

Glucose tablets, 29, 107
Goalkeepers, 40, 88, 93–5
Grassburns (abrasions), 40, 45
Groin strains, 53

Hamstring muscle, cramp, 60; loosening up, 54; tear, 49
Hand injuries, 92; abrasions, 38
Hangover, 105

Head injuries, 96
Heart attack, 103
Heel, pain in, 69
Hydrogen peroxide, 41, 112

Infection of skin wounds, 41
Inversion injury of ankle, 73

Jaw injuries, 99

Knee injuries, 81–90; cartilages, 86; ligaments, 85; strapping, 89

Ligaments, definition of, 9; ankle, 72; knee, 82
Loosening up, 49

Medisport, 12, 111, 114
Mouth injuries, 98
Muscle injuries, tears, pulls and strains, 48

Nose injuries, 98
Nutrition, 29, 106

Obesity, 30
Osteopaths, 21

Pharmacists, 22
Physiotherapists, 18, 115
Pott's Fracture, 77
Pre-match preparation, 104–108
Prevention, 25–38; of ankle injuries, 80; of foot problems, 63; of goalkeepers injuries, 88; of muscle injuries, 51; of skin wounds, 40–6
Psychological aspects of injury, 6
Pulse counting in training, 34
Puncture wounds, 45

Quadriceps, muscle, 84; loosening up exercises, 53; rehabilitation, 88; tear of, 46

Red Cross 17, 23, 115
Remedial Gymnasts, 18, 115
Rib, broken, 103

Salt deficiency, 30
Shoulder injuries, 91
Smith and Nephew, 12, 111, 114
Sportsystems, 114
Sterile dressings, 43
Stiffness, 58
Strapping, ankle, 15, 76; knee, 89; muscle, 50; principles, 14

Teeth, broken, 99
Tetanus, 43
Testicle, injury to, 102
Treatment bag, 110

Unconsciousness, 96

Verrucas, 66

Warming up, 52
Wrist and forearm injuries, 92.